Make Your Home in My Love

Make Your Home in My Love

Live in My Joy

BY

Catherine Skinner Powell

FOREWORD BY

Tilden Edwards

To Arnold,
May your dance of
mutual love with God bring
you both much joy,
Your sister in Christ,
Catherine

RESOURCE *Publications* • Eugene, Oregon

May, 2021

MAKE YOUR HOME IN MY LOVE
Live in My Joy

Resource Publications
An Imprint of Wipf and Stock Publishers
199 W. 8th Ave., Suite 3
Eugene, OR 97401

www.wipfandstock.com

PAPERBACK ISBN: 978-1-5326-8404-3
HARDCOVER ISBN: 978-1-5326-8405-0
EBOOK ISBN: 978-1-5326-8406-7

Permission from Fred Bock Music Company to use the lyrics by Mark Hayes' "To Love Our God."

All Scripture quotations, unless marked otherwise, are from the New Revised Standard Version Bible, copyright © 1989 National Council of the Churches of Christ in the United States of America. Used by permission. All rights reserved worldwide.

Scriptural quotations marked MSG are taken from *The Message*, copyright © 1993, 2002, 2018 by Eugene H. Peterson. Used by permission of NavPress. All rights reserved. Represented by Tyndale House Publishers, Inc.

Scriptural quotations marked TPT are taken from The Passion Translation, copyright © 2017, 2018 by BroadStreet Publishing Group, LLC. Used by permission. All rights reserved. ThePassionTranslation.com.

Cover artwork by Miyoung Paik. Used by permission. All rights reserved.

Manufactured in the U.S.A.   10/23/19

This is dedicated . . .
to the One I love.

To the Great Whisperer,
You are my strength.
Thank you for your gentle teaching, even up to today,
that I might learn to let go, yet some more,
receive your light,
make my home in your love,
and follow with joy
as you lead this dance of mutual love.
Amen.

I am the spreading vine and you are my branches.
As you live in union with me as your source,
fruitfulness will stream from within you,
but when you live separated from me,
you are powerless.

John 15:5 (TPT)

Contents

Foreword

— TILDEN EDWARDS —

WE LIVE IN A time of broadscale rediscovery of depth in the Christian spiritual journey, found in Scripture, many great spiritual exemplars in history, and in evolving personal experience. Embracing that depth involves a willingness to go the distance in trusting God's abiding love, a willingness to let that love further transform us into an abiding mutual indwelling, empowering the overflow of that love through us into the life of the world.

Catherine Powell has been deeply involved in that rediscovery for many decades. I came to know her when, in the early years of her yearning for greater depth, she participated in the Shalem Institute's eighteen-month extension program for the enrichment of people called to be spiritual companions for others—the historic ministry of spiritual direction. She founded her own center in South Carolina, The Anchorage: a Contemplative Community, where she has provided retreats and spiritual guidance for both clergy and lay people up to this day.

This book offers the choice fruit of her foundational learnings about the lifelong spiritual journey of recognizing God's love for us and the world, letting go of illusions and willfulness, seeing with the eye of the heart, intimately abiding in Christ, and bearing the authentic fruits of this path in the ways we are called.

Catherine gives steady emphasis to fostering our mutual indwelling in God as the ground of everything in our lives. As she puts it in relation to ministers, "Not only (does) God love them, but God wants to live life with them, to participate in their ministry and in their family, and especially in their own private times of prayer." Christ is the vine, and we are the branches who need to turn to the vine in a mutual exchange of love, and to live from that abiding in all we do.

This book is for those who yearn to live more fully from such mutual indwelling. I am one of those people. Some time ago, at the end of my daily prayer time, I was surprised by an inner voice that simply said, "Love me." I took that as the gracious One's voice. It has stayed with me steadily ever since. I keep answering, "I want to love you," or "I do love you," or "Our love is one love." What is it to love God, Creator, Christ, and Holy Spirit? Since God *is* love, then when I love God, I love Love. I'm being asked to recognize and embrace that Love's hidden presence in myself and in everything and everyone I encounter. I'm then actively abiding in Love, mutually indwelling in Love, loving in and with God's Love. It's not my autonomous loving; it's a shared love, a "we" love, "God in me" love. This is not a steady awareness, but an erratically growing one.

Catherine brings to this subject the historic experience of six great "heroes of the faith": Augustine, Bernard of Clairvaux, Catherine of Siena, Ignatius of Loyola, John Calvin, and Teresa of Avila, all of whom express the vital importance of a mutual love relationship with God. Although I am familiar with some of the writings of all these spiritual illuminators, I found what she says about each of them (devoting a whole chapter to each) to be a wonderful reminder of their stories and wisdom, and to add some of their valuable insights that were new to me.

The author brings to bear a historic way of describing a process of spiritual growth, reflected in the life and writings of each of these six outstanding Christian figures: dimensions of purgation, illumination, and union, to which she adds a fourth: God-guided action in the world.

In her final chapter she invites the reader to create a rhythm of life that includes spacious periods of time with God, in God, alone—times to listen more fully to "the Great Whisperer" in whom we live and move and have our being. At the end of each chapter she has well-worded questions for the reader's reflection.

I found Catherine's words full of wisdom, grounded in her own experience, in Scripture, and in the writings of God-inspired spiritual guides in Christian tradition. Anyone who reads this book will likely find affirmation and help for fuller life in God's abiding love, where we find our true home.

Preface

THIS BOOK WAS WRITTEN for the specific purpose of encouraging and inspiring those who wish to go deeper in their faith journey and reclaim the centrality of their love relationship with God. This honors the first and greatest commandment, which is found in both the Old and New Testaments. My hope is that with an increased awareness of this mutual love relationship with God, as God's sheer gift, that there would be more joy in ministry and, more importantly, more joy in life. The book is therefore titled *Make Your Home in My Love: Live in My Joy.*

In many years of offering spiritual direction and leading retreats, I have developed a deep compassion for pastors, priests, chaplains, and lay leaders, all of whom give so much of their time and talent to others, to the church, and to God. It is not unusual to hear such devoted men and women agree that they often feel like a dog at a whistlers' convention with so many people wanting a piece of them. Realizing that there are other similarly demanding vocations, this book is for all who long to live and serve God and God's people from a place of abiding in Christ. Perhaps others will draw thirst-quenching water from this well too.

We all benefit from hearing how much God loves us. But it may be that those ministers who serve so faithfully hear it less than anyone, and they may be the ones who need to hear it most—not only that God loves them, but that God wants to live life with them, to participate in their ministry, in their family, and especially in their own private times of prayer.

To ground our reflection in Scripture, John 15:1–11 provides the key metaphor from the last discourse of Jesus before his crucifixion. Jesus is the vine and we are the branches; apart from the vine, the branch can do nothing. There is a mutual exchange going on in the vine and branch, the sap and nutrients passing back and forth. In the same way God wants to be the supply, the source, in a mutual exchange of love, an intimate encounter of the finite with the infinite. We are invited to abide in God and live in that space, returning love to God in response to God's love for us.

We will look at the writings of several heroes of the faith: Augustine of Hippo, Bernard of Clairvaux, Catherine of Siena, Ignatius of Loyola, John Calvin, and Teresa of Avila, to glean from their thoughts and lives the importance of a mutual love relationship with God. We will use a process of spiritual growth as a descriptive tool: the Classic Three Ways, which include the purgative, illuminative, and unitive ways dating back to around 500 CE. I have added a fourth way, the unitive/active way. From that holy place of mutual love, action springs forth. The unitive/active way is participatory, humankind working with God however God leads. Consider what Maureen McCabe says at the end of her book about stages of prayer in the writings of Bernard of Clairvaux: "Our interior lives do not all begin and end in the same way . . . But cycles of growth are inevitable and within these cycles are landmarks experienced by all who are willing to pass through and not around them."[1]

Not being aware of any writing that encourages putting the highest priority on this love relationship with God, as illustrated in The Classic Three Ways Plus One, I offer this book to provide some encouragement to meet this sensed need. This book suggests that this mutual love relationship is the key for all of life, not just for ministry (because that would be using God as a means to an end). But the end is first and foremost this mutual love relationship with God, resulting in ministry as fruit, as a by-product, but first resulting in a joy-filled life.

1. McCabe, *I Am the Way*, 106.

For those who desire a more intimate relationship with God, the last chapter includes an invitation to create a rhythm of life that includes time with God away from all the distractions. The hope is that together with God's leading, the reader might encounter God more fully and live and love in and from that place in God's heart. God can help each of us discover the rhythm that is best: awareness momently, brief pauses throughout the day, quiet days, week-long retreats, even month-long retreats. The Anchorage: A Contemplative Community for All welcomes the opportunity to accompany men and women on directed retreats, or in monthly spiritual direction, or to point them toward similar nearby resources.

The anthem text below says it well.

To Love Our God
By Mark Hayes. Text: John Parker.

Where does the wind come from? Where does it go?
Blowing north and south; how does it know?

The rain flows gently to the sea, yet the sea is never full.
How can these things be? How can these things be?
How can they be?

Humanity works hard to make a name toiling in the sun,
yet nothing gained.
We all return to dust from whence we came.
All is empty, all is vain.

To love our God, the reason we live;
To love our God, the highest call.

Nothing satisfies our soul, gives life meaning, makes us whole.
For this purpose we were made, to love our God,
To love our God, the reason that we live is to love our God,

To love our God![2]

2. Hayes, "To Love Our God."

Acknowledgements

THIS BOOK IS BORN with a multitude of contributors especially since it is the culmination of thirty years of listening, processing, and formation. My formational family includes many who are not listed, and I'm more grateful than words can say to those who have spoken care and wisdom into my life. I decided not to include all the authors who have shaped me; just too many.

I'll begin with my spiritual directors over twenty-six years of monthly visits: Sr. Helen Godfrey OSC, Abbot Stan Gumula, OCSO, and Susan Sihler who introduced me to Teresa of Avila back in 1992. Next, the Jesuit Center for Spiritual Growth in Wernersville, PA, where I made the thirty-day Spiritual Exercises and then annual eight-day retreats for about twenty years. Many on the staff were helpful but I must name Kathryn Fitzgerald as she was my spiritual director for the exercises and most of the shorter retreats. She served on the advisory team of three for my DMin project which was the beginning of this book. My monthly spiritual direction peer group that began in 1993. I thank the Shalem Institute for Spiritual Formation where I first met "my people" at a silent retreat with Jerry May in 1991. Their Spiritual Guidance Program was timely and most formative. All who visit monthly for spiritual direction (directees) have heard and responded to much of this in conversation, and I'm grateful. Some of the pastors who helped form my faith with their wisdom during many of those thirty years are Hardy Clemons, Michelle McClendon, and Jeff Rogers.

In 1998, I founded The Anchorage: A Contemplative Community for All, responding to a call on my soul. The Anchorage Desert Day and Clergy Day participants have served as my test group for the content as I've been through almost all the chapters with them at our bi-monthly gatherings. The Anchorage Kanuga Retreat leaders and participants have helped to shape this book as we used the content for weekend retreats in 2018 and 2019. The Anchorage current Servant Leaders (Board) have encouraged my writing of this book. Grateful for all the Servant Leaders since 1998, for your generous giving of your time, talents, and treasure. One person gets credit for keeping The Anchorage alive around my cancer treatment, though she would give the glory to God: Peggy Dulaney, a beautiful soul who lives and loves in God. For all who receive The Anchorage quarterly mailing, "Depth Soundings," especially those who have written articles over the years.

For the book writing process itself, three folks were most hands on, offering writing suggestions: Steve Doughty, Claire Bateman, and Phil Krey. Phil read every chapter as I turned my DMin project into a book. His encouragement kept me going. Fil Anderson, Margaret Benefiel, Bob Hussey, and Walt McCandless provided lists of those who might be interested in using this book as a resource, a great marketing help. Bill Dietrich, Molly Marshall, and Marjorie Thompson, thank you for your endorsement in writing and in your lives. Merwyn Johnson, my systematic theology professor, encouraged me by believing that participation with God is an important and rarely named truth. Thanks to Tilden Edwards for living his life in God's love and writing the Forward with such understanding of my passion for God's invitation to all. And Emily Callihan, copy editor with Wipf and Stock, not only improved the punctuation and grammar, but also helped me say what I wanted to say. Thank you!

Melody Fifer is a friend who has loved me for over fifty years. Words cannot convey the gift she is to me.

The one who has carried the load with me daily is my dear husband Skeeter, who could not be a better encourager. His giving me space when I needed it and listening to my processing with a knowing nod from time to time, without giving advice, was exactly what was needed. THANK YOU!

Heartfelt gratitude and love for each of you.

And of course, most of all, our triune God, participating with me, leading this mutual dance of love, to birth this book. To God be the glory!

Introduction: The First and Greatest Commandment

WHEN YOU HEAR THE phrase "love of God" what comes to mind? Is it God's love for us, or our love for God? Just for fun I began asking folks this question as I was gathering thoughts about this topic. Everyone I asked said, "God's love for us," except for one person who asked, "Isn't it both?" It's expected that we would think of God's love for us first, as that is the foundation for any love that we have. Not to argue with that, but with other loves it often goes the other way. If we were to ask about love of children, or love of friends, we would most likely say, "Our love for them" not vice versa. So, I'm wondering if the first and greatest commandment, loving God with all of who we are, is central to our faith.

The common tendency is to move quickly to the second commandment, "You should also love your neighbor as yourself" (Mark 12:30), because we know, or at least we think we know, how to do that. It is tangible. We know about foot washing, visiting the sick and the imprisoned, and giving water and food to the thirsty and hungry. It is rare to raise the question, "What does it mean to love God? How does one do that?"

In addition, for many people not just the concept but also the experience is lacking—the experience of both God's love for God's creatures, and of each creature loving God in return with God's own love. At the outset, there is a gap between encountering God's love and finding words to talk about the encounter. So, the first challenge becomes discerning how to communicate this first and greatest commandment.

Many say that loving your neighbor *is* the way to love God. And that is one way. But there is so much more! And if that were all that Jesus meant with his response, why did he say there were two commandments? Loving God as the first and greatest, and loving neighbor as second? Might he have said more clearly that the first and greatest commandment is to love your neighbor? But he did not. The first and greatest is to love God. And the second is like it. His words imply that perhaps it is impossible to truly love neighbor without loving God. Love of neighbor is only authentic with pure motives when it flows from the love of God within us. So, as God leads, take a deep breath, and ask for the grace to learn how to love God. First let God love you, and then with "fear and trembling" let yourself be opened to experience what it means to love God with all your heart, soul, mind, and strength.

Does all this talk about loving God, about encountering the Living God, bring on some discomfort? We may be able to blame the Age of Enlightenment that taught us to value only what could be measured and analyzed, and we may have become a civilization that is more head than heart in our relationship with God, even within the church. It is a disservice to the world, especially the world of believers, to praise analysis and efficiency while rejecting love and intimacy. It is time to learn from our heart again, knowing that it, too, is a gift of God, to be honored and valued. Gerald May wrote a compelling book, *The Awakened Heart: Opening Yourself to the Love You Need* about this love relationship with God. In it, he wrote that if we need to choose between efficiency and love, always choose love.[3] When I tried to share this with someone, the only word I could re-call was "efficiency;" I could not even remember the word "love."

> *Caution! Opening yourself to loving God*
> *will transform your life!*

Though the intention here is to focus on our love for God, at the deepest level, our love and God's love for us are connected.

3. May, *Awakened Heart*, 4.

We may like to take credit for "loving God" as though it were our own idea. However, we are reminded by many writers throughout the centuries that our only hope of loving God comes from God. God's love for us comes first; only then are we able to love God. Kierkegaard says it well in his prayer, "Thou hast loved us first many times and every day our whole life through."[4] Even when we decide to pray it is because God has awakened our thought and nudged us. This understanding is our foundation, or even deeper, is the root, for our consideration.

Many believers do not give this first and greatest commandment the full importance, the central place in the journey of faith. Some may even be asking, "Why all the talk about loving God? What difference does loving God make in everyday practical living out of faith and ministry?"

Consider this writing attributed to Pedro Arrupe, former Jesuit General:

> Nothing is more practical than finding God,
> that is to say:
> than falling in love
> in a quite absolute, final way.

> What you are in love with,
> what seizes your imagination,
> will affect everything.

> It will decide
> what will get you out of bed in the morning,
> what you will do with your evenings,
> how you spend your weekends,
> what you read,
> who you know,
> what breaks your heart,
> and what amazes you with joy and gratitude.

---

4. LeFever, Ed. *Prayers of Kierkegaard* 14.

Fall in Love,
stay in Love
and it will decide everything.[5]

According to Arrupe, the one most practical thing we can do is to fall in love with God, by God's grace, in response to God's love for us. Living in this love relationship is our best hope for our lives not to mention our ministries, and it just may be the best hope for the world. Might be helpful to repeat that last sentence. *Living in this love relationship is our best hope for our lives not to mention our ministries, and it just may be the best hope for the world.* This truth applies to anyone anywhere, not just to some elite group.

5. Burke, *Arrupe*, 8.

1

The Vine and the Branches

THE SCRIPTURES AFFIRM NOTHING is more practical than loving God. Of the many Scripture passages that encourage this love relationship with God, John 15, especially the first eleven verses, does this with a clarity from the very heart of the teaching of Jesus. These verses are part of the "farewell discourse" of Jesus in the Gospel of John, chapters 13 through 17, just prior to his arrest and crucifixion. In chapter 13, Jesus knows that his death is near. After supper, before the festival of the Passover, Jesus washes the disciples' feet as a poignant illustration that the master is not greater than the servant. At the end of chapter 13, Jesus cautions Peter, after Peter's bravado statement that he would die for him, that Peter will betray him that very night. Chapter 14 follows with more teaching including the promise of the Holy Spirit and many verses about the love relationship with God the Father. Whether chapters 15 through 17 were inserted later, as some scholars believe, these chapters pulse with the gravity of Jesus' approaching death. It is within this context that Jesus speaks of the vine and the branches. These words are central to all that has come before in Jesus' ministry and to all that lies ahead for his followers.

The very structure of John's writing accents the importance of what Jesus is saying. Frequently in his Gospel, John employs a two-fold structure: the primary level of meaning concerns Christ, and the secondary relates to the disciples. Examples abound especially in the "I am" statements. The words are used over and over. Not only does Jesus say, "I am the bread of life," but he then goes on to say, "He who comes to me shall not hunger" (John 6:35). Again, "I am the light of the world" and "He who follows me will not walk in darkness" (John 8:12). It is a beautiful dance, if you will, of Jesus with the believers, a participation of the divine with the human, the infinite with the finite. At the outset, notice that throughout, though the word "participation" itself is not used, there is much reference in the words of Jesus to a concept that is today growing in prominence: participation of God in the life of the believer. This two-fold, participatory structure appears at the very beginning of John 15 and continues throughout. "I am the vine, you are the branches. Those who abide in me and I in them bear much fruit, for apart from me you can do nothing" (John 15:5). Lest we get ahead of ourselves, let's return to verse 1 for other important insights, but keep your awareness sharp for this two-fold structure, as it is critical.

The significance of the "I am" statements Jesus makes must be mentioned briefly. The use of these words would not have been lost on the Jews. It was the name God gave to God's very self when encountering Moses in the burning bush, and the meaning carries much weight. It means that God was, is, and will be. The verb denotes being, very being itself, before all time and continuing until after all time. Jesus' use of this term in describing himself contributed to the charges of blasphemy that Jewish leaders held against him. To say "I am" was in effect saying "I am God." Of course, that is exactly what Jesus was saying.

Further strengthening Jesus' words here is the specific metaphor he employs. Metaphors run rampant in both Old and New Testaments, and one of the oldest and most common metaphors for Israel is the grapevine, with God as the vine grower who tends the vine carefully, needing to prune, sometimes drastically. The Greek root for pruning means "cleanse" and involves cutting back to the bare stem. As verse 2 says clearly, God, the vine grower, prunes so that the plant will bear more fruit, cutting off completely those that are dead, bearing no fruit.

Those who have spent time trying to grow plants, especially flowering plants, become aware of the need to prune. In 1999,

Eugene Peterson, at a Bowen Conference at Kanuga Conference Center in Hendersonville, NC, told a story about watching his neighbor prune his rose bushes. He said that it looked as if the man might be killing them, cutting them back so far. Peterson did not prune his but enjoyed the luxurious growth throughout the year. The next year, at the time for the blossoms to appear, his own bushes were big but produced very few blossoms, while his neighbor's rose bushes were full of blossoms. It was a lesson learned. The pruning was essential for blossoms to occur.

It is the same with disciples. Jesus wants the disciples to catch the idea that though they have already been pruned to some extent by leaving their belongings and other ambitions behind, and they have born some fruit, there will be more pruning necessary in order to bear more fruit. Jesus is saying he is the true vine, he is the true Israel, and his followers are to remain in him. He is saying more clearly, using this metaphor, the most important message he must leave with his disciples. He is "speaking of the intimate relationship with him that they are to enjoy, and (so to speak) to cultivate."[1] Jesus is offering this to everyone; therefore, we must be ready for the pruning knife as well in order to bear fruit of good quality and in abundance.

Of all that is involved in growing healthy plants—the planting, tending, watering, getting rid of bugs, harvesting—the only part that is mentioned in this allegory is the pruning. Why would this be? Is it because this is the one part that would be questioned as being good for the plant? From all outward appearances, the pruned plant is dead or at least dying. No sign of life appears. So it is often with disciples, in the day of Jesus and today. This passage encourages those who are undergoing difficult times in life to know that with God as the vine grower, all difficulties can be used for God's purpose in some way. That God only prunes the branches that are already producing fruit indicates that God's pruning is a blessing, though it may not appear to be so at the time. Building trust in God, regardless of appearances, is an underlying theme.

---

1. Wright, *John for Everyone*, 70–71.

While leading a retreat using this material for content, I became aware of a situation that had not occurred to me before. One of our retreatants was grieving her son's death a few years earlier and was doing some beautiful work, trusting God with the healing. It dawned on me that she or others in similar situations might interpret a tragic event such as the death of a loved one as God's pruning. We talked about it and I was relieved that she had not seen it as God's hand, but it prompted me to provide these words to those who have lost loved ones. I asked a wise friend, Phillip Krey, for input and his words say it well. "God is definitely not pruning when people die. God is there suffering with us. I think pruning communicates shedding things that would separate us from God or keep us from being disciples. It is not about people dying, but our dying to ourselves and our wants as opposed to our needs." God's pruning relates more to our calling and is more about letting go of those things, perhaps overcommitments or useless growth, that might hinder us from abiding in God.

The invitation that Jesus gives his disciples in this discourse, to abide in him, is the crux of the passage, and perhaps the main hope of the gospel message. Jesus then adds "as I abide in you." He expresses a desire for a true mutual indwelling: God in the human, the human in the Divine. The metaphor is clear in the vine and the branches; there is an exchange between them—the sap, the nutrients, the water, the energy freely flows from one to the other. Without this mutual exchange between the vine and branches, there is no fruit. So it is with God and disciples. Without a mutual indwelling, a flowing back and forth of love, there is no fruit. The words "because apart from me you can do nothing" are startling, especially for any who have placed all their hope in their own efforts.

Living in that love relationship with God is the invitation. But an invitation to what? There are so many answers to that question, but the primary one according to Jesus seems to be in order to bear fruit and to have full joy. He also says abiding in that love relationship with God glorifies God and enables us to love others.

Could there be a better reason for loving God? Not only is this a blessing for one's own life and one's ministry, it even glorifies God! Is it even possible to be part of transformational ministry without loving God? Might it be that this love relationship, abiding in God, is the key to whatever else happens? The model used in this book is *descriptive* not *prescriptive* and happens only by God's grace. The importance of taking time to note that the work is truly God's throughout always moves one to greater humility and dependence on God.

This fruit is usually interpreted one of two ways: either fruit of the Spirit growing in the disciple, an interior fruit, or the fruit of ministry, an exterior fruit. While the second interpretation has merit and is of value, it is a distant second to the first meaning. The fruit of the Spirit growing in the disciple must come first and be deeply rooted in the disciple in the unitive space with God, so that then they are available to be used in any exterior ministry.

It is not uncommon to read the word "if" as conditional in many passages when the better interpretation often is "when." In an example from John 8:31, Jesus says, "If you continue in my word, you are truly my disciples; and you will know the truth and the truth will make you free." It just does not resonate as truth in keeping with the rest of the gospel to see this as a conditional statement. Jesus is not setting up an "if/then" condition as some sort of prerequisite task to perform. He is more clearly saying, "When you continue . . . then, at that time, you are my disciples and you will know the truth." It is a given—again, more of a descriptive term than a prescriptive term. At the point when the person is in the word, then the rest naturally is happening. God is not withholding some favor, waiting on humankind to get it right, but rather freely giving to all, no strings attached, wanting us to live the gospel fully.

So, in the same way with John 15:7, "*If* you abide in me" is not a condition set up by God for us to obey in order to receive the glorious benefits of God's giving. Rather the word "when" is the more accurate meaning. When you abide in me, and my words abide in you, ask for whatever you will, and it will be done for you. It makes so much sense to see that whatever we would ask for when we are in God, and God's words are in us, would be in keeping with what God already wanted.

The words of Jesus confirm this meaning, as he goes on in verse 8, "My Father is glorified by this, that you bear much fruit and become my disciples." Nowhere is there any indication that the person will be glorified, just God. In the same way, when the branch bears the fruit, can the branch take any credit? No. It was said clearly that without the vine, the branch could do nothing. But it takes both the vine and the branch. God chooses to work *with* us—a participation of the infinite and the finite in the production of fruit. In looking at a vineyard, would anyone say, "Look at that beautiful branch?" No. One might say that the fruit is beautiful, or perhaps that the vine is lovely, while completely ignoring the branch, allowing for the humility that is just the truth of it to develop. That phrase comes from a conversation years ago with my spiritual director, Sr. Helen Godfrey, a sister at the Monastery of St. Clare in Travelers Rest, South Carolina. I had asked her to talk with me about humility, just to give me some insight. Her reply was, "It's just the truth of it." I was waiting for more, but she was through. When we look at God and look at ourselves, it is so clear, it is just the truth of who we are: we cannot help but be humble.

The vine, Christ, is producing the fruit on the branch. The branch is grateful for the invitation to participate in producing beautiful fruit, but not wanting any honor or attention. This symbolism continues to teach on so many levels, now teaching about true humility. When we know it is Christ doing the work, we can enjoy the process, just being a branch. Is that perhaps a good prayer for a disciple? "Lord, teach me to be content to be a branch."

And even beyond that, Jesus wants a mutual indwelling in love—but not just to produce fruit! It is much more than producing fruit; it is about loving each other. The ongoing exchange of love with God is the end, with a lovely by-product of fruit. *When you keep my commandments, you will abide in my love, just as I abide in my Father's love.*

We may ask how *do* we abide in Christ? We must, by God's grace, be people of prayer and worship both in our corporate lives and in our own intimate private lives. We must be sure to be in touch, in tune, with Jesus, knowing him and being known by him. It is an intimate experience, being a branch on the vine. Abiding in Christ, being a branch attached to the vine, entails two themes: we are to abide in God's love and to bear fruit.

Moving on to verse 9, this love relationship is emphasized even more. "As the Father has loved me, so I have loved you; abide in my love." Another interpretation is "remain in my love." In *The Message*, Eugene Peterson paraphrases John 15:5 as "make your home in my love."[2] Hence the title of this book. It is all grace, a gift from God. You may be asking, "What is my part?" This prayer can be helpful in many situations. The answer: our part is to surrender and just be.

This section, dwelling on the metaphor of the vine and the branches, brings us the closest to the meaning of the first and greatest commandment. This mutual encounter of love, of living in love, provides an unfailing illustration of what it means to love God with God's very love. "[It is] the most complete expression of the mystical union between Christ and the Christian in this Gospel. It combines the thought which Paul expressed in the figure of the body and its members with the peculiar emphasis which John lays on love as the chief mark of this inward fellowship. Continued dependence upon Christ is the condition not only for fruitful service, but even for continued life."[3]

The mutuality of love is the key, taking time to dwell in that love. The more we are aware of being with Christ, the more we will be like him. The more we are aware of being in his love, the more we will love as he loves. In the Gospels we see that Jesus took time to be with the Father, withdrawing to a solitary place, a place of quiet away from the crowd, free of distractions. What an encouragement to us to have permission, and an example, in this production-driven culture, to sit with God in quiet to replenish our souls. We are encouraged to go on retreats in order to listen for God's voice so that we are more inclined to make time for this

2. Peterson, *The Message*, 1469.
3. Howard and Gossip, "The Gospel," 717–18.

constant contact when we return home. It may mean rearranging the day, even changing some long-held habits, so that this time is always honored.

George Maloney, a Jesuit familiar with the spiritual exercises of Ignatius and the eight-day retreats that have grown up as a shortened, modified version of the exercises, has written a book, *An Eight-Day Retreat: Alone with the Alone*, as a model for a solitude retreat. In it he often refers to the first few verses of John 15 as an example of this deep connection, this intimate union with God. Here are a few quotes. "The more we can live in God's love by finding him very close to us in every moment in every activity, the more meaningfulness will come to our life. This loving God is not far removed from the monotony, the slow growth, even the apparent setbacks, the pains and the sufferings of our every day. He is "inside," present in his loving activities, seeking only to share himself more and more completely since that is the nature of free love."[4]

The words "command" and "commandment" are prevalent beginning in John 13:34 continuing through chapter 15. The words are not new. They are found often in the Old Testament. Yet Jesus keeps calling it a "new commandment" that he is giving them. Loving others is not new. What *is* new is the command or commandment to love others as Jesus has loved them. The way Jesus loves *is* brand new: washing their feet, talking about dying in order to live. And Jesus says he has loved them as the Father has loved him. Again, it is the mutual indwelling, the abiding in Christ, as he abides in us, as the Father and Christ abide in each other, that is the only way to love as Christ loves. From this inward union with Christ we are told that kingdom fruit will grow, especially in our own lives, that we will become more like Christ, and that we will bring glory to God.

We can see in verse 10 that the same words are repeated to emphasize how essential this understanding is. When reading the passage aloud, one becomes even more aware of the repetition, and the point is driven home that it is both keeping the commands and abiding in the love of Christ. We are to do what Christ does as he

---

4. Maloney, *Eight-Day Retreat*, 131–32.

THE VINE AND THE BRANCHES

keeps his Father's commands and abides in his love. It is always the same pattern; we are to do as Christ does, allowing his relationship with the Father to live in us. There is no other way, and he often says so. Our only hope of living in this incredibly intimate relationship with Christ is that he is doing it in us! We as branches draw nourishment from the vine or we will be barren and wither.

The symbols of Christian Eucharist, the bread and wine—common, everyday elements from the table of our Lord during his life on earth—bring this passage to mind. Our understanding of the sacrament is enhanced as we recall the vine and the branches and affirm again that we must drink from the Lord, that our branch must draw our nourishment from the true vine in order to survive.

It may come as a surprise in verse 11 that Jesus says, "I have said these things to you so that my joy may be in you, and that your joy may be complete." He speaks of joy being complete again in John 16:24 and 17:13 as the reason for all that he has said. This phrase needs careful attention. It is exciting to know that if we are living in the love of Christ, then his joy will be in us, and our joy will be complete. One way to interpret the joy is that of a bride being brought to her husband, Christ.

A former abbot of Mepkin Abbey, Father Christian, ninety-eight at the time of this writing, says that the most perfect expression of Christianity is joy. This resonates as true, if the joy results from this abiding in Christ, living in this mutual exchange. If a Christian is joyful, it does not mean that he or she is not a sinner. On the contrary, he or she is a *redeemed* sinner.

In *The Message*, Eugene Peterson provides meaning as he says, "I've told you these things for a purpose: that my joy might be your joy, and your joy wholly mature." It makes perfect sense that if we are living in this intimate, loving relationship with Christ, as modeled by his relationship with the Father, then we would also have his joy. To go through each day with a fully mature joy means that the circumstances of life do not move us from this place of joy deep inside, where we live, where we abide in Christ, but rather that these tough circumstances deepen that love relationship. "Just as Jesus imparted peace to the troubled hearts of his followers, so now he inspires them in the hour of gloom with his own radiant joy. Joy is henceforth a note of the true church."[5] There is much more that could be said about the joy of the Christian life, but for now consider this thought from *The Interpreter's Bible*.

> We are the children of joy, and the first Christians literally were so. And if that is no natural or fitting definition of us now, then we are less than fully Christian, and are missing something that Christ has to offer us that would make us so.[6]

Bringing us back now to the choice of this passage to help us better understand and live the first and greatest commandment, we must underline the importance of this mutual indwelling. It is this intimate exchange of love that brings us the joy. According to Bernard of Clairvaux (more in chapter 4) this joy is the reason God asks for our love. It is not for some egotistic reason, but because God knows that precisely when we love God, by God's grace, then we are our most joyful.

A personal story belongs with this chapter. I had taken copious notes, studied, and read for about two years in preparation. Pastor friends had provided resources for me, and all seemed ready to put it on paper. I gave myself the summer to get it done. Every time I tried to begin writing, nothing would come; it was like a block of some kind. Perhaps with my role at The Anchorage, the fact that I did very little preaching made it more difficult? My chemo brain due to cancer treatment over the previous two years was fuzzy at best and downright blank at times.

It was mid-August. I was sitting in my prayer chair, praying, and it became clear that I was not able to write this important piece of the book. I cried out to God, "I can't do this. Please help." It was as if I heard God saying, "Bingo! I can help! I thought you'd never ask." I didn't hear an audible voice, but a very clear sense of God's presence was there with me. As I smiled, even laughed a little, I asked God how this worked. What I sensed was God saying,

5. Howard and Gossip, "The Gospel," 721–22.
6. Howard and Gossip, "The Gospel," 722.

"You'll need to get up and go to your computer." It reminded me of when God said to Abraham, "Get up and go" and the next sentence reads, "So Abraham got up and went." So, I got up and went to my computer. I sat down and began to key. The time flew by. In about three and a half hours I had keyed about seventeen pages with footnotes and all. I remember saying to God, "You are really good at this!" And wondering since this was about Scripture if this might be an exception . . . wishing I had written all the other chapters this way. What a gift! What a joy!

What was even more remarkable to me was that we were living the content of the passage of Scripture. God and I were being the vine and the branch! God was giving me a living example of how this works, of how much God wants to be asked for help. Since that summer day I have asked for help much more quickly. And my sense is that it always makes God smile.

It was evident that God only used what was already inside me, nothing I had not read, studied, and understood. Therefore, the work really was a project we *both* did. I was a willing participant with God. It continues to come clear to me that participation is how God longs for us to live, participating with God as we go through this life, listening for God's nudges and doing it together.

Reflection with the Vine and the Branches

Settle In

Take a few moments to settle in. Look around. Listen. Notice what you notice. Feel the chair supporting you and your feet on the floor. Get comfortable. Stretch a bit if that helps. Take a deep breath or two to let your body help your mind slow down. Be aware of God's face turned toward you in love right here, now. *Behold God beholding you in love.* When you are settled in, move to the options below, whichever ones speak to you.

1. How does this invitation to intimacy feel to you? Is it welcomed with open arms, or maybe a little intimidating? Is it

a new thought? Or perhaps newly received? As you open yourself even more to God's love, ask God's Spirit to bring something to mind that God might want you to recall. Write whatever comes as you ponder this together.

2. Enjoy some time basking in God's love. And as it moves through your body, and you feel the strength of it, ask God to help you return it back to God and then overflow to others as God leads. Then you might ask what it is God might want you to note about it. Write as led so you can recall it later.

3. Become more aware of how often your heart is turned toward the fruit of your branch, rather than the root. Ask for the grace to be aware of when your heart is tempted to turn from the root to the fruit.

4. Close by expressing your gratitude to God if it is true for whatever God has shown you during this time of quiet. End by finding some way to tell God of your love. A simple "I love you" will do. If you would like to write, please do.

2

The Classic Three Ways Plus One

A VERY BRIEF HISTORY of the Classic Three Ways finds its origins traced back to Pseudo-Dionysius the Areopagite who wrote around the year 500. He wrote as if he were a contemporary of Paul, using the pseudonym Dionysius the Areopagite mentioned in Acts 17:34. He was actually a disciple of Plotinus and Proclus. Because it was about a thousand years before the false identity of Dionysius was discovered, his writings greatly influenced St. Bonaventure (1217–1274), who in turn influenced many others down through the centuries.

One twentieth-century writer, influenced by Bonaventure, is Benedict J. Groeschel, a Franciscan friar. He brings an updated understanding of the Classic Three Ways to our time with clarity, so his words will provide much of our introduction to this ancient process. The Classic Three Ways include the purgative, illuminative, and unitive ways. As said before, this model is not *prescriptive*, but *descriptive*, as believers who long to deepen their love relationship with God move through these ways, or stages. Awareness of where one is on the journey may not matter, but the fact that this path has been common for many may reveal some new insights.

A few words of preparation are essential before we move into detailed definitions and examples of the Classic Three Ways. The process is complete in itself; nothing is lacking. However, prior to the first way, the purgative way, there is a realization that takes place within the believer. It is a given that God's love is constant for every person in the world. God is forever loving us fully, and in each moment, providing inflowing love on us and in us. Something stirs and awakens the believer to God's enormous, constant, undeserved, unconditional love. This awareness is in response to God's love, but God will not force the awareness, so the believer must be willing to wake up. And God gives us chances throughout our lives, again and again, with hope that we will wake up to know that we are loved.

When God's light can get through the chink in our wall, we can still ignore it if it seems too overwhelming. But eventually as God pursues us, in many cases the believer is moved deeply and, with a grateful heart, enjoys being loved. There is a response of gratitude. The believer is in awe, noticing the contrast between God and self. This awareness is the preparation required for the beginning of the Classic Three Ways.

A helpful conversation with Father Stan Gumula, OCSO, who was then Abbot of Mepkin Abbey (a Trappist Monastery in Moncks Corner, South Carolina), revealed his observations over many years that a deepening in a believer's love relationship with God often comes as a breakthrough experience, usually resulting from a crisis of some kind. And it is rarely smooth, moving gracefully from one stage to another, but rather a bit of a jolt. In the crisis, God prompts the person to respond with a mutual exchange of love, and when the person does not refuse, a breakthrough occurs. But because of God's generous grace, the person can refuse the mutual exchange of love and miss the breakthrough. This breakthrough language, noted in detail by Rosemary Haughton in *The Passionate God*, seems to correlate with this moment of awareness.

Please do not misunderstand. Of course, God can do whatever God wants to do. God can turn any process upside down and inside out. That said, this order of the ways that are described here is the usual order. It is worthwhile to present this model for the journey of faith that has been happening since the days of Jesus, though many variations occur.

The integration of spirituality and psychology is evident in the three ways, even though the process was being lived and experienced long before the word "psychology" was coined. The admonition to know oneself is not new and has been encouraged over many centuries. Teresa of Avila (more in chapter 8) was adamant that believers know themselves. She encouraged making two lists: one illustrating how much we are loved, how precious we are to God, and the other showing that we are sinners in need of a redeemer. She emphasized the truth of both lists at each moment in our lives. Yes, *even then*. And isn't that the message so prevalent in the Gospels, in the words of Jesus, and throughout the first testament, the Scripture Jesus knew from his childhood, especially as found in Isaiah and the Psalms?

Benedict Groeschel writes primarily from the position of integrating psychology and spiritual development. He has extensive experience working with Christians on the journey of faith in his profession as the director of spiritual development of the archdiocese of New York. His interest in the Classic Three Ways and his conclusions come from his observation of individuals seeking this deeper love relationship with God. Now let us look closely at what this model reveals. "To the degree that a person responds to the awakening—for response is always necessary—life will be changed. It may require years for an awakening to 'take hold' and it may recur frequently. When at last it is accepted, the individual must begin to put his or her life into some relationship with that call."[1]

The purgative way includes a time of purging, purifying, and shedding. It is a process of letting go, of emptying—not only emptying the hands of whatever one is holding tightly, but at a deeper level, emptying the self, the false self. The purgative way often begins when life is not going well, and one discerns that for life to go well, there is a need for some change. Usually one begins by changing the outer situation, and sometimes that seems to be enough for the time being. However, when old habits continue or recurring "self" themes become evident, the pain may lead one to a greater letting go. Rarely does one choose this acknowledgment, and many go through life willing to bear or numb the pain rather than deal with it.

1. Groeschel, *Spiritual Passages*, 74–75.

One wise woman, while attending a beach retreat with The Anchorage, said that "letting go" may be a good way to sum up the spiritual journey; more and more letting go of our way as we ask for God's grace to make more room within us for God's way, to live in union with God. This description is the purgative way simplified.

For those who are intentional about a more holistic way of relieving the pain, rather than just the Band-Aid approach (at which our culture excels, with excessive materialism and instant gratification, expecting things to satisfy), the purgative way opens the soul to the next way, the illuminative way. Groeschel goes into much detail about the first darkness of the purgative way, describing the struggle and the temptation to turn back. However, those who persevere make it to the second stage.

According to Groeschel, there are two main reasons to stop and not enter the illuminative way. One is the fear of a life without self-seeking, and the other is a fear of finding fulfillment and real happiness. The old is more familiar even if it is a miserable way to live. The price of change can be too high.

And now, because of the emptying, there is space for something new. The illuminative way is an opportunity to learn, to grow, to see with the heart, to listen for God. One is more aware of a desire to know Jesus better, to see him more clearly, love him more dearly, and follow him more nearly. The spiritual life in this stage flows as a response to the love of God received, rather than as a chore or duty. "The Christian in the illuminative way lives on Scripture and is fed on the writings of the saints. Reverence and awe are growing in the inner life and the soul is now seen not so much as a shadow being but as the inner place where the Trinity abides in glory. As the illuminative way proceeds, a silence and calm envelop the individual. This is reflected mostly in prayer—'the prayer of quiet'—wherein listening brings more answers than speaking."[2]

Contemplative Outreach, a centering prayer organization founded shortly after Vatican II by Fr. Thomas Keating and other Trappists, has popularized centering prayer, also called

2. Groeschel, *Spiritual Passages*, 83.

contemplative prayer, or quiet prayer. This popularity reveals that souls are moving toward the illuminative way. Fr. Keating became aware of the great hunger for quiet prayer, demonstrated by the number of people, Christian and non-Christian, turning to Zen Buddhism and other Eastern religions because they were drawn to this practice of quiet prayer. He reclaimed it as part of our own Christian tradition, and now there are centering prayer groups in churches and elsewhere all over the world. Our distracted culture knows this need. The current word in vogue is "mindfulness." A search for that word on Google brought up many computer apps ready to be used to help provide mindfulness. Businesses are encouraging quiet moments and classes on mindfulness.

The lyrics of an old hymn come to mind as it asks God's Spirit for illumination. The illuminative way is not rational or cognitive knowledge, but perhaps more like a light going off inside. It may even bring us to silence. It's a deep knowing, in that we know that we know.

The illuminative way reveals the beginning of the process of finding the living water that will quench the thirst, something (or Someone) that will scratch the itch. There is a quiet gentleness about the person in this phase, and a deep openness to God.

The unitive way is difficult to define. Discussion of the unitive way moves us to the depth and primary focus of this book. The unitive way is experienced more than explained, described more than defined. Put most simply, it is the union of the Creator with the creature, not the meshing or mixing of essences so much as the joining of wills. The prayer of Jesus in the Garden of Gethsemane comes to mind, "nevertheless, not my will but yours" (Matt 26:39). It is in this unitive space that the fruits of the Spirit are formed in us.

> A short summary of the unitive way is not possible. Words fail and thoughts evaporate as one attempts to describe the experience of union with God which comes to the very few who arrive at this way of infused contemplation. Without being spectacular, the unitive way is also totally absorbing, like love's quiet joy. Yet when one encounters the unitive way in its most common form,

among the elderly who live lives of peaceful gratitude to
God, it seems to be a simple childlike hymn of praise.
In all cases, it is a movement whose source is beyond all
human origin or limitation.[3]

It is evident that Groeschel's work is formed by Dionysius's
thought, as he implies that only a very few are privileged to experience infused contemplation. Many disagree and insist that this way
is open and available to all, for it is God's desire for each person to
know this way of being. The three steps in the Classic Three Ways
are experienced as cyclical and are often repeated throughout our
lives. It is not static but a journey. Though union with God in love
and friendship is the most highly valued experience of the Christian faith and fulfills the first and greatest commandment, the purpose of that union is not only to please God and for humankind to
be fulfilled. There is more.

Once the creature has tasted divine union with the Creator,
then, as a natural effect, the mutual love between Creator and creature overflows to others almost indiscriminately. The Classic Three
Ways, while complete in themselves, do not address this natural
overflow from being in the unitive way (being at home in God's
love) to loving God's people as God leads with God's love. There is
no way to be in a truly deep, intimate love relationship with someone and not care about their concerns. So it is with God. If we are
willing to surrender our need for control and yield to this intimate
love relationship with God, then of course we will love whom God
loves and be moved to action. Hence another "way," a fourth way,
is born, creating the Classic Three Ways Plus One.

This active way is more accurately called the unitive/active
way. Adding the word "unitive" to "active" highlights the difference
between moving into action from an ego-driven, self-centered
place with little or no dependence on God, and being active from
within a place of dependence on God, with awareness of God.
When active from within that unitive place with God, it is God's
interests and God's energy at work, even God's resources, which

3. Groeschel, *Spiritual Passages*, 86.

do not run out. It may look the same from the outside, but from within it is a different awareness.

This unitive/active way is not the love of just the creature. No, it is life-changing love, effective because it is God's love in the creature providing the power, the life. As discussed earlier in chapter 1, loving the neighbor from that place of union is described well in one of the most challenging passages in Scripture. It seems that sometimes repetition is of value, so we note that in John 15:5 Jesus says clearly that unless the branch is attached to the vine, the branch can bring forth no fruit. "I am the vine, you are the branches. Those who abide in me and I in them bear much fruit, because apart from me, you can do nothing!" The awareness of the inability to do anything without being attached to God as the vine is what drives and sustains the new way of living.

As the creature grows in awareness of God's power and grace, as it becomes more conscious, always as gift, sheer gift, from God, then the creature lives and loves from that place, participating with God in whatever God is doing, as God leads. While that deep, indwelling love (*agape* love), God's love, is actively loving others (*caritas* love) through one who is in the unitive/active way, then there is an abundance of time, energy, joy, and peace, enough to share.

However, if the creature begins to try to do the work, the loving and the serving, from the creature's own store of love, joy, peace, and strength, then the value, the quality, and the effectiveness of the ministry changes. The work no longer gives life. Eventually, the creature at best can serve with great effort and little fruit, or at worst, the creature crashes and burns.

So, the question is: what needs to happen at that point? The creature needs to return to the Creator, to honor again its dependence on God alone to do the work. One suggestion is to return to the purgative way. Usually there is more to purge, to empty, to surrender, to let go. It seems to be the nature of the creature to try to find answers to life's questions in the shallow cisterns of Jeremiah, rather than in the deep living water of God as revealed in Christ. Perhaps asking, "What am I grasping too tightly?" or "What has replaced you, God?" would provide some insight.

Adding a new "way" to the Classic Three Ways, a Fourth Way, the Plus One, is not really a new thought. The idea is implied, if not explicitly stated, in many familiar writings on the spiritual journey, as illustrated in the following chapters. These descriptions and definitions provide a good starting point to better understand this graced process. But lest the reader miss the main point, it is all about God: to be with God, in God, as a branch attached to the vine, grateful moment by moment for whatever it is that God wants to do with us. It is not that we are instruments in God's hands to get the work done, but that God chooses us, by name, as individuals, to participate with God, as God's chosen, in the work God wants to do in us and with us in the world.

Here's an illustration that may clarify this concept. It involves a small cup and a good-sized pitcher full of water. As I pour the water into the cup, the cup fills and begins to overflow. I describe this as God pouring God's love into us, filling us full to overflowing. It is a John 15 way of serving, of doing ministry. Then I take the cup out from under the flow of the water. The pitcher continues to pour. But out from under the flow, the cup must be jiggled and sloshed so that some water will flow out, so that some ministry or service (fruit) will occur. Eventually there is no water left in the cup. Even as I vigorously shake the cup, no results. There is nothing flowing forth. Then I direct my attention to the pitcher. It is still pouring! As I move the empty cup back under the flow, the cup fills up again and overflows freely with abundant water, enough for all. Without being under the flow, without being filled up first, all we have to offer others is ourselves, and that is not much, especially when compared to the life-changing eternal results of being filled with God's love. The statement "Apart from me you can do nothing" rings true.

Top View of the Classic Three Ways Plus One Diagram

Please refer to this diagram that may help with the concept of this flow. Though the historical terminology for the Classic Three Ways according to Dionysius (purgative, illuminative, unitive) are descriptive and resonate well with the academic community, when speaking with the general public about this process, often their eyes begin to glaze over. To resolve this problem, I've added words that may be more familiar. Allow me to orient you to the diagram.

Please begin with the center. The name of Christ in all caps indicates that the center of all of life is the Lord Jesus Christ. It may remind you of the rose windows from the Middle Ages, during the French Gothic period, with a most famous one being in the Notre Dame Cathedral in Paris, France. Rose windows, also called Catherine Windows, and often the center of the "Wheel of Fortune," always had Christ or the Virgin Mary and Christ in the center, inspiring viewers to consider what it might mean to make Christ the center of one's life. Note that long before the televised game show, this wheel was a symbol of the capricious nature of fate, and the Greek goddess Fortuna would spin it at random. The outer rim of the wheel had the words "I reign" at the top, "I have reigned" on the right side, "I have no kingdom" on the bottom and "I shall reign" on the left side. For believers, the encouragement is that staying in the center with Jesus, we can be aware of the rising and falling of fortune and remain in Christ, held and loved.

Moving to the "Start Here" suggestion, one experiences an awakening to either a longing for God, or an awareness of being loved by God, or both. It can be experienced as a need or as a restless heart. This time of awakening can lead to an invitation to let go, to shed whatever is no longer necessary or helpful, during a time of emptying. Paradoxically, it is God who truly does the emptying once a degree of willingness is established. We cannot do it by ourselves. As that emptying process occurs, there is now space to receive illumination, to see anew, whatever it is God might want to reveal. Next, God invites us into union with God's very self, an intimacy that is beyond words. God provides great delight in this place of mutual love, interior spiritual fruit grows, and because the beloved loves whatever the Lover (God) loves, there is a heart's desire to become love and to serve others, to let the overflow of this mutual love pour out to the needs of others. Doing the work *with* God, participating, is like a dance. Yes, a dance with God, being led at each turn: now a pause, now we move more quickly, all completely depending on God's leading.

When this glorious way of living and serving remains fully dependent on God, when we make our home in God's love, it can go on forever. However, it is easy for us to forget our need for God, like Peter looking at the waves when he walked to Jesus on the sea (Matt 14:30). When we realize we have moved out of the flow of God's leading and providing, when we become aware of being burned out because we are doing it all by our own strength, hopefully we discern, sooner rather than later, that it is time to make a change. Perhaps what is needed here is more letting go. We might want to ask, "Am I holding something too tightly that is not of God?" The timing is ripe to move back to the purgative way, the way of letting go, of letting God empty us. It is not just returning to where we were before. It is a letting go, it is purgative, but always at a deeper level, deeper into the love of God.

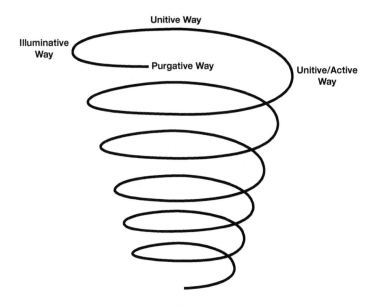

Side view of the Classic Three Ways Plus One Diagram

    The diagram with the side view reveals that the process is a spiral not just a circle. It is a gift of God that we reenter the process at a level of deeper awareness of being in Christ each time. This growing awareness continues for our entire lives. It is God's heart that leads us.

    There are four simple prayers that accompany The Three Classic Ways Plus One. Beginning with the purgative way, or the way of letting go, and moving around the circle with Christ always at the center, as the focus of life: "Empty me." "Illumine me." "Fill me." "Lead me." These prayers and other more familiar words flow around the academic words, with the hope of the process becoming friendlier, more welcoming.

In the next few chapters, we will illustrate the Classic Three Ways Plus One using the writings and lives of some prominent leaders in Christian history upon whose shoulders we stand. While there are many more heroes of the faith that we could include, from ancient times to today, in order to focus our study, we will spend time with Augustine of Hippo, Bernard of Clairvaux, Catherine of Siena, Ignatius of Loyola, John Calvin, and Teresa of Avila. Enjoy!

Reflection on the Classic Three Ways Plus One

Settle In

Take a few moments to settle in. Look around. Listen. Notice what you notice. Feel the chair supporting you and your feet on the floor. Get comfortable; stretch a bit if that helps. Take a deep breath or two to let your body help your mind slow down. Be aware of God's face turned toward you in love, right here, now. *Behold God beholding you in love.* When you are settled in, move to the options below. Select whichever ones speak to you.

1. Take a few moments to think back over your life, paying attention to the times you might call an "awakening" in your faith journey. Select one and write a bit about it, pondering what difference it has made in your life.

2. As you shift your focus to a season that was a time of shedding, a purgative time, a time of letting go, ask God's Spirit to help you recall. As one comes into focus, write a bit about it, noticing what was shed and what difference that made.

3. Now move to an illuminative time. Invite the Spirit to help you become more aware of a time in your life when you were learning new things—a time when there was light and "aha" moments because there was room to receive such insights.

4. This time turn your reflection to an instance, or even a season, that you might call unitive—a time of being loved by and loving God in a fuller sense than before. What difference did this make to your life of faith and to your life in general? Write about it with whatever words come.

5. Now reflect on a time of action—with or without God. Perhaps there are times of both. See if you notice the difference. Flesh out a time when you knew God was doing the work and you were participating with God. Ponder these thoughts with God and discern if you are willing, eager, ready to learn more about this.

6. Rest in God without words, opening to whatever God has for you.

7. If it is true, close your reflection time with gratitude for who God is and for what God has done, is doing, and will do.

3

The Classic Three Ways Plus One as Found in the Dolbeau Sermons by Augustine of Hippo

AUGUSTINE (354 TO 430) served as bishop of Hippo, a region in North Africa, and was a genius. His *Confessions* is the most widely known of his writings and arguably the primary classic of the spiritual life in the Western world. The prayer "You have made us for yourself, and our hearts are restless until they rest in you"[1] has been quoted often, as it indicates the underlying cause for our lack of satisfaction with anything, for any length of time. At times I've been a bit angry about this truth because restlessness has been so prevalent in my own life. Once we begin to live into the truth of this prayer, we become more in touch with God's first and greatest commandment as our best hope. If we can turn our desire toward God, everything else falls into place. "Strive first for the kingdom of God and his righteousness and all these things will be given to you as well" (Matt 6:33). The "restless heart" phrase relates to the awakening but continues beyond that throughout our lives.

The Augustinian tradition in spirituality was the common heritage of the Christian laity and of many religious orders in medieval times as well as today. It's been said that during the Protestant Reformation both the Protestants and the Roman Catholics were quoting Augustine to prove their points. The title "Doctor of the Church" was created to give Augustine recognition, as his

---

1. Augustine, *Confessions*, 2.

26

understanding of theology was significantly broader and deeper than that of others.

A brief timeline of his life might help make Augustine more personable, but know that all the detail is available in his *Confessions*. He was born in Thagaste in North Africa and was schooled about twenty miles away. His family saved so he could go to school. He moved to Carthage to complete his law education as a teenager. He had a son with his longtime girlfriend at eighteen, the same year his father died.

Augustine read Cicero's *Hortensius*, which led to an intense search for the truth and a deep interest in philosophy. He began teaching in Thagaste, then in Carthage, and then in Rome.

His mother, Monica, had prayed fervently for him to become a Christian and especially prayed he would not go to Rome because of all the temptations there. But it was in Rome that he became a believer at the age of thirty-two! We can see that sometimes it is best when God does not answer our prayers the way we would like. The next year, in 386, he was baptized along with his son.

Augustine returned to Africa after Monica's death and was appointed assistant bishop to Valerius. The next year, Valerius died and the care of the diocese fell to Augustine. He wrote his *Confessions* over the next few years. His writing became an instrumental way for him to teach, and he wrote until his death in 430 when Hippo was attacked by the Vandals.

He is known for his incredible ability to communicate complex theology and what today is called psychology. Yet, the symbol the church identified with him was a heart, because love was at the heart of his teaching and his life. God's love for us comes first, of course. Only then are we able to love even God. Love was central, was the rock, the anchor not only for Augustine's thought in sermon, letter, and book, but for his life, for his relationships, for his ministry as bishop, until his death.

May we all be encouraged to reclaim the centrality of our love relationship with God, particularly listening for our part, asking, "How are we to love God?" Though our focus is on our love for God, we must begin by saying clearly that our love and God's love are intimately connected. Augustine said that it is God's love in us with which we love God in return. This understanding is our foundation, or even deeper, is the "root" of our consideration of what it means to love God.

In English we simply use the word "love" and may miss the nuances of the various Latin words for love (*agape, philia, eros, caritas, amor, delectio*, etc.). At the risk of oversimplifying, it may be that Augustine's *caritas*, the word he chose to describe love for God and neighbor, also included some of the dynamics of *eros*, a thirst for or need for another, and perhaps also *agape*, God's self-giving love to humankind.

For Augustine, if we love God well, then the love for others and ourselves just naturally follows. The word "second," as in second commandment, can be translated, "the commandment that follows." Similarly, if we love our neighbor well, then it is a given that we already also love God as the source of love.

We'll be using the Dolbeau sermons to flesh out Augustine's path of love for God. Thirty full or partial sermons were found in 1989. The manuscripts most likely date from around 1470. Scholars believe that Augustine delivered one cluster of them in late spring or summer in Carthage around 397 and others in late winter or early spring in 404, mostly in Carthage, but some in the upper Medjerda valley. They are called the Dolbeau sermons because François Dolbeau first perceived that these manuscripts contained sermons that were either totally unknown or had been known only in extracts up until this time. This exciting discovery has, in Dolbeau's words, "brought back the voice of a long-dead friend."[2]

One of the obvious benefits of having the texts of these sermons is that they do not have the errors common to those having many copyists, since they were not circulated much in the Middle Ages. There are at least three numbering schemes for Augustine's sermons, and we will use the Dolbeau sermon numbers, 11, 16, 19, 22, and 25, for scholars who might be interested.

God's love for us is the beginning place for Augustine. He quotes 1 Corinthians 4:7 asking the question, "What do you have

2. Brown, *Augustine of Hippo*, 444.

that you have not received?" We cannot love others, or even God, without first receiving that same love from God.

Augustine cleverly poses the question about the greatest commandment, asking how we can love God with all our heart, soul, and mind and have any love left over for the second commandment, for loving others and ourselves. Later he answers his own question by saying,

> So, don't be afraid that by leaving yourself nothing to love yourself with, you may perish. You won't perish because by loving God with your whole self you will be in a place where you can't perish. If you don't want to perish, take your place IN One who cannot perish.[3]

The key to all instruction about loving God, found throughout Augustine and more importantly in Scripture, is that we cannot do it on our own. We can only love God, ourselves, and others by loving with the love God has placed in us, the love by which God loves us. As the branch attached to the vine, we can love when we abide, make our home, in God, where love abounds.

However, since our love for God seems to be a passed-over doctrine, in our day at least, so much so that when we talk of the "love of God" we usually only think of God's love for us, hopefully Augustine's Dolbeau sermons will bring this invitation from God into a greater, or perhaps deeper, reality in our own lives.

While many ignore the concept of loving God today, it was not so for Augustine. His works teach it repeatedly. Not surprisingly, we find this topic prevalent in the Dolbeau sermons. Though Augustine preached these sermons early in his service as bishop, he was already very clear that we are to love and fear God throughout our lives because we cannot love perfectly. However, the more our love for God takes root, the more it grows, the more our fear diminishes. Augustine goes on to say, "[God] is on the lookout for the hearts of those who love him sincerely. He is asking to be loved by one whom he is not loved by."[4]

---

3. Augustine, *Sermons III/11*, 82.

4 Augustine, *Sermons III/11*, 289.

Don't miss Augustine's point here. He speaks powerfully to the relationship of love of God and neighbor. After reading Matthew 22:40, which says, "All the Lord's commands are fulfilled by this law of love," he goes on to say,

> Why were you stretching and straining through all the spreading branches? Hold onto these roots, and the whole tree is in your hands. The Lord as we can see, stated this very briefly; I, however, am obliged to say much more about these two commandments. Or perhaps I'm not obliged to, and what we have heard from the Lord is sufficient? Of course, it's sufficient, but not for everybody. You see, the greater people's minds, the more what is briefly said suffices them.[5]

This illustration shows Augustine's genius. Picture holding the whole tree! His logic was clear but arduous, starting with self-love, then moving to love of neighbor, coming back to loving God as the only way we can love others and ourselves. He asks,

> Why love something which you diminish by giving it away? Bring your neighbor whom you love as yourself to that capital good which is not diminished by any number of shareholders. The good which belongs in its entirety to each and every one, however many more come to possess it. Unless you love such a good as that, how will you ever love your neighbor as yourself? What is this good? You have it in the first and greatest commandment. You see, when you begin to love God, it is only then that you love yourself.[6]

Augustine's preaching is understandable so that people's hearts were touched and changed. It is as though Augustine heard God's heart. His understanding of love of neighbor and self-love provides us with a profound new way of seeing. The words of Augustine say it best:

> If that is what you love, what you really set your heart on, then I will entrust your neighbor to you, because I

5. Augustine, *Sermons III/11*, 78.
6. Augustine, *Sermons III/11*, 81.

can see where you are aiming at and wending your way
to. You will lead him there, nor can you lead one whom
you love as yourself anywhere else; you are now, after
all, also loving yourself. Love God, with all you've got;
with your whole heart and with your whole soul and
with your whole mind. In this way, in this way alone will
you love yourself, in this way alone can you love your
neighbor as yourself.[7]

The first "way" of the Classic Three Ways, the purgative way,
is seen clearly, as Augustine deals so honestly with his fallen nature, knowing there is no hope within himself. There is a deep
hunger in us for God, but we so easily mistake it for a desire or
need for so many other things or people. How many folks do we
know who are dealing with addiction? How many lives are de-
stroyed trying to ease this deep ache? Gerald May, psychiatrist
turned spiritual director, says that there is no such thing as an
addictive personality because these words describe us all. It is human nature. As said before, we are yearning for something we
know not what, and all the while it is God.

"There is absolutely nothing, in fact, that can satisfy you,
except God; nothing is enough for you, except God."[8] Early in
his career as a Bishop, Augustine preached this truth, central to
his theology. It was about the same time he wrote *Confessions*. He
continued to teach and live this truth all his life. God is enough—a
truth sorely needed in our world today.

Augustine sees this purging and shedding as ongoing, as we
are never through with discovering more places that need God's
healing. Augustine sees God's hand in it all as an act of great mercy,
and we are to appreciate it.

It's difficult for God not to find something in you that
calls for punishment. You are now rather pleased with
yourself. Well, God knows something which escapes
you, finds in you what you were hiding or perhaps what
you didn't even know about. So, let us love the work of

7. Augustine, *Sermons III/11*, 83.
8. Augustine, *Sermons III/11*, 85.

mercy, while our ills are being healed so that when our ills have been healed, our desires may be sharpened; being sharpened may they be satisfied and then face judgment with mercy. It is tiresome after all, that it should be without mercy.[9]

That last sentence prompts this humorous note from the translator, "A splendid understatement, surely uttered with tongue in cheek and a completely straight face."[10] Anyone trying to imagine what this work would be like without mercy would quickly see we would not survive it.

Augustine encourages us to hope in the Lord saying that the *summum bonum*, "highest good," is in the heart. He is revealing the contrast between our attention to "the many" and to "the single One." He says, "[We are] desiring many things, distracted by different pleasures, not seeking the one thing necessary."[11]

In a later sermon, he says it colorfully with a metaphor showing that this purgative way is about letting go of what I want so I can receive what God wants for me. "But you have got into the habit of finding enjoyment in these things, and when you start giving them up, the hunger caused by a habit broken off will cause you pain. But that's the harshness of the strong ointments with which eyes are cured. Accept the doctor's order."[12]

Again, Augustine teaches that it is God's initiative. He teaches from his own life, and what he says comes across as genuine. "Now though [God] in fact is offering himself, you there are looking for something else."[13] Augustine says, "Don't draw back from your God; love your God. You're always saying to God, 'Give me this or that'—say to God sometimes, 'Give me yourself.'"[14] Doesn't this capture it well? Of all the things we think we need, once we shed, once we let go, we begin to realize *God* is what we truly need.

9. Augustine, *Sermons III/11*, 85.

10. Augustine, *Sermons III/11*, 86.

11. Augustine, *Sermons, III/II*, 73.

12. Augustine, *Sermons III/11*, 376.

13. Augustine, *Sermons III/11*, 289.

14. Augustine, *Sermons III/11*, 74.

During the purgative way we see our own weakness. Augustine knows of what he speaks when he says, "To receive God's grace we must know our weakness."[15]

If we want to receive mercy from God, we are to rest in our weakness, our emptiness, open to God's revelation however it comes. "The inner eye of the heart needs to be cleansed in order to see the light of God."[16] Having let go of much in the process of the purgative way, the soul is now ready and open to receive from God whatever God sends. This empty openness is the beginning of the illuminative way.

In this phase, our hands are open and empty enough to receive something new. Augustine knows just what it is that we need. Our openness to God's love, our availability and receptiveness, is our part, and even that is by God's grace. Our part is not to study and grasp and understand so much as it is to be with; to receive whatever God has to offer; to receive God. After quoting part of Psalm 103, Augustine teaches these words of life.

> So, with our sins forgiven, our ills healed, our life re-
> deemed from decay, our crowns bestowed on us by
> [God's] mercy, what shall we be doing, what shall we
> have? Who satisfies with good things, not bad things?
> You will be satisfied with God.[17]

Augustine quotes Psalm 111:10, "Make your heart ready with fear to receive the seeds of charity," saying that the fear of the Lord is the beginning of wisdom, inviting his hearers to let go in order to make room for the new. Discernment is a necessary part of this phase. We need to "unknow" God or learn what God is not. These words of Augustine confirm the process in the Classic Three Ways.

> This is not my God, it is the work of God. When we see
> something lovely, look for the one who made it and tell

---

15. Augustine, *Sermons III/11*, 123.
16. Augustine, *Sermons III/11*, 267.
17. Augustine, *Sermons III/11*, 84.

yourself, God is not this. The inner eye requires an inner light to see by. The heart must be purified by faith.[18]

However, it is not unusual in the illuminative way for there to come a new awareness of something that needs to be purged or let go. Augustine offers us help first with words that define that situation and then brings us to a new place in our pilgrimage of faith.

So, we pray convert us (heal us), God of our healings. Before you heal us, we have our backs turned to you—and while we praise the bread—loss of appetite prevents us from receiving it. We enjoy the bread of life which came down from heaven, to the extent that our ills are cured. We are to enjoy the "bread"—Jesus. After praising it [Jesus] we eat it quietly because we love it, appetite restored, illness cured.[19]

The illuminative way is a time of seeing, of learning. In our trials, God is revealing not only God's love for us, but also our own love for God because *we* need to know that we love God; God already knows. We are encouraged to let our love be fully for God and only for God. We need to hear these words of Augustine today in our consumer-driven society. It is worthwhile to ask ourselves, how have we missed this teaching, even in seminaries?

If you love him, love him for nothing, freely. Love God freely. You see, if you love him on account of something else, you aren't loving God at all. You mustn't want him for the sake of anything else, but whatever else you want you must love for God's sake so that everything else may be referred to love of God, so that God may be preferred to other loves.[20]

In his *Confessions*, Augustine recorded a mystical experience with his mother, Monica, at Ostia, and wrote of his garden experience, when he heard children's voices telling him to take up (let

18. Augustine, *Sermons III/11*, 370.

19. Augustine, *Sermons III/11*, 122.

20. Augustine, *Sermons III/11*, 74.

go of control?) and read. His sermons follow the same theme and offer descriptions of the unitive way.

Of course, we cannot sustain this stage of union with God, but we are to desire it because God desires it. Augustine may have experienced this union with God during his later life more often than recorded, as he speaks quite often of soaring which resembles his experience at Ostia, where he and the Spirit soared.

> In order that this most delightful and surpassing and inexpressible Trinity may be loved, soaring beyond the universal creation which it initiated, completed, arranged, soaring beyond it altogether, the Spirit desires the hearts of lovers. You see, when you have soared beyond all changeable things, spiritual as well as material, you will come to the contemplation of the Trinity and you will drink from the same source as he drank from.[21]

Augustine was insistent that *in God* is where we are to live, and that the invitation is for all believers. Union with God means being in God as the branch abides in the vine, making its home there. Augustine says it well, "So let us believe in him, love him, in the sense of being incorporated in him by loving him."[22] In this unitive place the fruit of the Spirit blossom.

Now we consider a fourth way, the unitive/active way, as what must naturally occur when we are in God. When we are in this place of union with God, God, in delight, throws us back into the world to love as God loves, and we meet this gesture with the same delight. It is not even a conscious choice. It is a natural overflow from living in God's love to loving our neighbor and serving that neighbor as God leads.

We recall the two commandments set before us earlier. Augustine says that when we do not understand this concept, it is not that we love badly, it is that we do not love at all! He goes on to add that perhaps the reason we don't break the commandments against our neighbor (you shall not commit adultery, you shall not murder, you shall not covet, etc.) is because we are afraid of getting

21. Augustine, *Sermons III/11*, 288.
22. Augustine, *Sermons III/11*, 122.

caught, not because we love justice. Living for an audience of One comes to mind as we imagine hearing Augustine preach:

> One could have been enough, love your neighbor. But to prevent you from going wrong in loving your neighbor, because you were going wrong in loving yourself, the Lord wished to give the love you love yourself with a kind of mold in the love of God. Only then did God entrust your neighbor to you, to love as yourself. Let your real action take place inside you, take place where the one who can reward you can see you. That's where you must fight, where you must win. That, after all, is where you have the spectator that counts.[23]

Therefore, as we are rooted and grounded in God, we will love our neighbors and ourselves for God's sake, not out of some need to impress others or gain anything for ourselves. Our love for God is especially not in order to find favor with God. The love with which we are to love is God's love within us, and it is sheer gift because of who God is.

We are encouraged by Augustine to love and love well with God's love.

> So, if you love, love too the very thing you love with, and you are loving God. What you love with is charity. You love with charity, love charity, and you have loved God since God is charity and whoever abides in charity abides in God! Choose whichever love you like. You choose love of neighbor, it won't be genuine unless God is also loved. You choose love of God—it won't be genuine unless neighbor is also included tacitly.[24]

While scholars will continue to debate the use of the various Latin words for love, Augustine, especially in his later years, might have called for fewer distinctions, as he saw that they all originate in God. They are helpful when they do not distract us from the actual act of loving God in response to God's love and with God's love.

23. Augustine, *Sermons III/11*, 83.
24. Augustine, *Sermons III/11*, 84.

We are grateful for Augustine, for his brilliance, and especially for his heart for God. How encouraging that such a genius would be so in love with God. His deeply rooted love for God, overflowing from God's love in him, provides an explanation of why his works have had such a lasting influence. Is it our task now to receive God's love and then love as God loves, both God and then neighbor? What would the world be like?

Reflection with Augustine

Settle In

Take a few moments to settle in. Look around. Listen. Notice what you notice. Feel the chair supporting you and your feet on the floor. Get comfortable. Stretch a bit if that helps. Take a deep breath or two to let your body help your mind slow down. Be aware of God's face turned toward you in love, right here, now. *Behold God beholding you in love.* When you are settled in, move to the options below.

1. You are invited to ponder this Augustine prayer: *"You have made us for yourself and our hearts are restless until they rest in you."* Take a few moments to let it sink in. Where does it apply to your life? How do you see the truth of it? Look over your life and notice when you may have tried to calm your restless heart with things other than God.

2. What do you discern about this quote of Augustine's? "If that is what you love, what you really set your heart on, then I will entrust your neighbor to you, because I can see where you are going. You will lead [him/her] there, nor can you lead one whom you love as yourself anywhere else; you are now after all, also loving yourself. Love God with all you've got; with your whole heart and with your whole soul and with your whole mind. In this way, in this way alone will you love yourself, in this way alone can you love your neighbor as yourself."

3. Augustine is clear that we cannot sustain this unitive/active way with God, yet we are still to desire it because God desires it. Recently in a workshop it was said that the truer a truth is, the more difficult it is to hear it. It just demands too much of us—for example, the paschal mystery, to die to oneself. Take a little time to let the Spirit remind you how you might be self-sabotaging your union with God because it just feels too big. Write whatever is helpful.

4. Take a little more time with the diagrams as God leads. What else is for you there. Write something to recall it later if you like.

5. Spend the rest of your reflection time with God, asking God for the grace to be open to receive whatever God might want to give you. Ask God to help you become more aware of what you truly desire. Bask in God's love; let your God love you.

6. You may close your reflection time with gratitude if that is true for you.

4

The Classic Three Ways Plus One as Found in *On the Song of Songs* by Bernard of Clairvaux

THERE ARE MANY WRITINGS that provide information about the early life of Bernard of Clairvaux, but they usually begin by saying that there is very little historical information about him. He was born in Fontaine-lès-Dijon in 1090 to a family of minor nobility of Burgundy, France. His father was a knight and his brothers expected to follow him.

We know little of Bernard's childhood, as the only account written was by William St. Thierry who knew Bernard after he became abbot of the Clairvaux Cistercian monastery. William wrote without Bernard's knowledge and never consulted him. It is a theological treasure but hardly on objective biography.

Suffice it to know that he was gifted intellectually and at the age of twenty-one decided to become a monk at Cîteaux, France. He brought many family and friends with him, revealing his natural leadership ability. He became their abbot because of his authentic love of God. Much could be said of his accomplishments, but perhaps most important is his persuasive way. People trusted him. At the time of his death in 1153 his order included 330 houses or monasteries across all of Europe. Between eight hundred and nine hundred monks had been part of the community at Clairvaux before he died. He became the spokesman for a revival of monastic life in an age when the spirit of the religious life was endangered.

Bernard expected the strict observance of Benedict's Rule. His love of God and the centrality of humility in his life drew scholars and laymen as well as monks.

It seems essential to begin our search for the Classic Three Ways Plus One in *On the Song of Songs* by restating that God's love for us is always first. We read in Scripture (1 John 4:10) and in theologians such as Kierkegaard that "God has loved us first."[1] As said previously, though the main emphasis in this book is our love for God, we must always begin with God's love for us.

Bernard speaks of the soul in reference to Song of Songs 3:1, "Let her seek him as she can, provided she remembers that she was first sought, as she was first loved; and it is because of this that she herself both seeks and loves."[2] And in the next paragraph, referring to the same verse, "This is what you are urged to do by the goodness of him who anticipates you, who sought you, and loved you before you loved him. You would not seek him or love him unless you had first been sought and loved."[3]

In *The Mystical Theology of Saint Bernard*, Etienne Gilson writes of another important clarification.

> If God is charity, and if charity must needs be in us if we are to know God, then charity must of necessity be given by God. There we have the origin of the distinction, so important in St. Bernard, between the charity which is God, and the charity which in us is the "gift" of God. This distinction is suggested by the verse that declares that charity comes from God: *"Caritas ex Deo est"* (1 John 4:7).[4]

Since God loves us first, our love for God is necessarily secondary, and as much as we would like to take credit for it, it is not ours to take. However, that does not mean that it is unimportant! On the contrary! It is God's highest goal for us, to love God.

1. Lefevre, *Prayers of Kierkegaard*, 13.
2. Bernard, *Song of Songs IV*, 191.
3. Bernard, *Song of Songs IV*, 191.
4. Gilson, *Mystical Theology*, 22.

> Love is the only one of the motions of the soul, of its
> senses and affections, in which the creature can respond
> to its Creator, even if not as an equal, and repay his fa-
> vor in some similar way. For when God loves, he desires
> nothing but to be loved; since he loves us for no other
> reason than to be loved, for he knows that those who love
> him are blessed in their very love.[5]

In *Athirst for God*, Michael Casey offers Bernard's theology
of human nature to provide the anthropology of desire for God.
Other authors writing on Bernard have said the same, but Casey
says it particularly clearly.

> Because God formed us with a capacity for and compat-
> ibility with himself, it follows that any human movement
> toward God is a direct result of this gift. It is not a con-
> sciously willed initiative from the human side, nature, as
> it were, apart from grace, but a grace-inspired assent to a
> pre-elective tendency of being which impels him toward
> final glory. The significance of this approach is that it
> elevates desire above the level of an affective experience
> of yearning for the absolute and accords it an ontological
> reality; it is the movement of an incomplete being toward
> its divine completion.[6]

Having established the centrality of our love for God in Bernard's theology, we will now turn to the understanding of the Classic Three Ways Plus One as found in his *On the Song of Songs* as a
way of looking more deeply into this love relationship. And note
that when Bernard uses the phrase "love of God," most often he
means our love for God rather than God's love for us. It is time to
reclaim this as central for believers today.

Bernard begins his *On the Song of Songs* with an explanation
of why he is preaching sermons on this book of the Bible, saying,
"The instructions that I address to you, my brothers, will differ
from those I should deliver to people in the world."[7] So we see at

---

5. Bernard, *Song of Songs IV*, 184.

6. Casey, *Athirst for God*, 60.

7. Bernard, *Song of Songs I*, 1.

the beginning that his audience is his brothers in the monastery. He takes his lead from Scripture as he does throughout all his writing, and quotes Paul saying, "We have a wisdom to offer those who have reached maturity" (1 Cor 2:6), and invites the brothers to "be ready then to feed on bread rather than milk."[8]

The Anchorage recently held a retreat on "Prayer: Experiencing the Intimate Encounter" led by Duke Walker of The Inner Hue. Near the end my comment was "This is not Prayer 101; it is a graduate course." So it is with the Song of Songs.

Because of the maturity of Bernard's audience, we will find fewer references to the purgative and illuminative ways and far more references to the unitive way, with a natural overflow to the unitive/active way. With that said, our search for purgation in *On the Song of Songs* requires some teasing out. Bernard is not explicit about the need for the purgative way in these sermons, partly because by the time one is ready for the Song of Songs one most likely has already undergone some intense purgative experiences. However, Bernard and other mystical writers are quick to say that this progress from awareness of God's love for us, through the purgative, illuminative, and unitive ways is rarely, if ever, a one-time passage. We continue to cycle back through the purgative way as we become aware of other false-self issues, other sin, and areas in our lives that we need to let go. Yet remember that it is not a repetition per se. It is a spiral. Each time, we are more deeply aware of the love of God.

In his first sermon, Bernard indicates that the brothers must have already done some purgative work.

> Now, unless I am mistaken, by the grace of God you have understood quite well from the book of Ecclesiastes how to recognize and have done with the false promises of this world. And then the book of Proverbs—has not your life and your conduct been sufficiently amended and enlightened by the doctrine it inculcates? These are two loaves of which it has been your pleasure to taste, loaves you have welcomed as coming from the cupboard of a

8. Bernard, *Song of Songs I*, 1.

friend. Now approach for this third loaf that, if possible, you may always recognize what is best.[9]

Bernard's reference to Ecclesiastes here suggests Scripture that would be helpful for the purgative way, as an emptying, and his reference to Proverbs suggests Scripture for the illuminative way, as a new heart seeing, leaving the Song of Songs to be mostly about the unitive way. This third loaf, as described by Bernard, is the meat, the bread, the solid food, "a more nourishing diet for those who are spiritually enlightened."[10]

Yet there are a few references to sin, to the purgative way, particularly in the earlier sermons.

> Since there are two evils that comprise the only, or at least the main, enemies of the soul: a misguided love of the world and an excessive love of self, the two books previously mentioned can provide an antidote to each of these infections.
>
> Taking it then that these two evils have been warded off by the reading of those books, we may suitably proceed with this holy and contemplative discourse which, as the fruit of the other two, may be delivered only to well-prepared ears and minds.[11]

Bernard expounds on the "kiss of his mouth" from Song of Songs 1:2 over three entire sermons (sermons 2, 3, and 4) coming back to it again in two later sermons. He ends sermon 4 with these words, "I have spoken extensively . . ."[12] indicating that he knew he had gone on. The three kisses as brought to life by Bernard provide a structure for us as we consider Bernard's use of the Classic Three Ways.

This graced process is a movement toward union with God, but Bernard warns that we are not able to jump right to the "kiss of his mouth." However, in great humility, he indicates that there is a

---

9. Bernard, *Song of Songs I*, 1.
10. Bernard, *Song of Songs I*, 1.
11. Bernard, *Song of Songs I*, 1.
12. Bernard, *Song of Songs I*, 24.

way of progress toward the kiss of his mouth, beginning with the kiss of his feet, which relates to the purgative way.

> I should like however to point out to a person like this that there is an appropriate place for them on the way of salvation. They may not rashly aspire to the lips of a most benign Bridegroom but let them prostrate with me in fear at the feet of a most severe Lord. Like the publican full of misgiving, they must turn their eyes to the earth rather than up to heaven. Eyes that are accustomed only to darkness will be dazzled by the brightness of the spiritual world, overpowered by its splendor, repulsed by its peerless radiance and whelmed again in a gloom more dense than before.[13]

And speaking of the woman in Song of Songs 1:5, Bernard says that the skill which enabled her to accomplish this change was that "she wept bitterly, she sighed deeply from her heart, she sobbed with a repentance that shook her very being, till the evil that inflamed her passions was cleansed away."[14]

Still in the same paragraph, Bernard reminds us of the dialogue with Simon about the woman with the alabaster jar. Jesus asked him who would love more, the one who was forgiven a small debt or the one who was forgiven a large debt (Luke 7:43). Awareness of our indebtedness, our sinfulness, does not repel us away from our loving God, but brings us ever closer as we begin to dare to believe that we are fully known and fully loved. That we are forgiven the larger debt, that we are aware of our most grievous sin, only increases our love for our Lord, in gratitude and awe.

> Prostrate yourself on the ground, take hold of his feet, soothe them with kisses, sprinkling them with your tears and so wash not them but yourself. Thus, you will become one of the "flock of shorn ewes as they come up from washing." But even then you may not dare to lift up a face suffused with shame and grief, until you hear the sentence: "Your sins are forgiven," to be followed by

13. Bernard, *Song of Songs I*, 17.
14. Bernard, *Song of Songs I*, 17.

the summons: "Awake, awake, captive daughter of Sion, awake, shake off the dust."[15]

Bernard warns that if we become attached to an inappropriate object, we must bring it under control. And adds, "Rightly, then, does she renounce all other affections and devotes herself to love alone, for it is in returning love that she has the power to respond to love."[16] Michael Casey offers a vivid description of Bernard's concept of the need for the purgative way.

> This involves a vigorous renunciation of alternative attractions in order to give oneself entirely to the pursuit of the one thing necessary. What is, perhaps, most difficult is relinquishing a hold on those sensible attachments which were permissible and perhaps even helpful at a previous stage of growth and the recognition that each phase has its own specific demands. Thus, the process of ordering the affects continues throughout life.[17]

Casey also says that the soul must submit to the painful process of pruning, not knowing how long or extensive it will be. There is a further problem. It is not only beginners who make beginnings.

So, returning to the kiss of the feet as our first kiss, we become aware of our tremendous need and are filled with great sorrow for our sins and failure to let God be God; yet often we are still holding on to all that we hold dear in this world, filling our hands so that we cannot receive anything from God. For the person in such great awareness of need, in this step of forgiveness, Bernard gives each of the two feet that we kiss a name. The names are "judgment" and "mercy." Bernard is clear that only God can help us let go. "O Wisdom, reaching mightily from end to end in establishing and controlling things, and arranging all things sweetly by enriching the affections and setting them in order!"[18]

---

15. Bernard, *Song of Songs I*, 17.
16. Bernard, *Song of Songs IV*, 185.
17. Casey, *Athirst for God*, 105.
18. Bernard, *Song of Songs III*, 37.

Compunction, a word used often by Bernard, is an essential part of the purgative way. By "compunction" he means the awareness of guilt that often leads to contrition. The admission and confession of sin is motivated by God's love and grace, but there is still a sting to it. Tears usually accompany purgation and are a good sign that there is no hardness of heart, which resists grace. Thus, compunction is a work of love and enables the soul to grow strong and prepared for the next stage.

According to Casey again, Bernard recognizes that there are different stages in the spiritual pursuit which must be understood and their sequence respected. The Classic Three Ways is an example of the stages that often result in union with God. As we continue through this process, we leave the purgative way and move into the illuminative way.

The illuminative way relates to the next kiss after the kissing of the feet. As a reminder, closely following this purgative way, there is a gratitude for sins forgiven, and the penitent is encouraged to aspire.

> You will please him much more readily if you live within the limits proper to you, and do not set your sights at things beyond you. It is a long and formidable leap from the foot to the mouth, a manner of approach that is not commendable. His hand must be your guide to that end. First it must cleanse your stains, then it must raise you up. How raise you? By giving you the grace to dare to aspire. On receiving such a grace then, you must kiss his hand, that is, you must give glory to his name not to yourself.[19]

"Experience" is a key word for Bernard. He praises the Song of Songs as the book of Scripture that "stands at a point where all the others culminate."[20]

> Only the touch of the Spirit can inspire a song like this, and only personal experience can unfold its meaning. Let those who are versed in the mystery revel in it; let

19. Bernard, *Song of Songs I*, 19.
20. Bernard, *Song of Songs I*, 6.

all others burn with desire rather to attain to this experience than merely to learn about it. For it is not a melody that resounds abroad but the very music of the heart, not a trilling on the lips but an inward pulsing of delight, a harmony not of voices but of wills. It is a tune you will not hear in the streets—these notes do not sound where crowds assemble; only the singer hears it and the one to whom he sings—the lover and the beloved.[21]

This illuminative time is a seeking time. It is a time for new insights gleaned from listening, reading, and trying new ways of living and loving. Recalling the *Rule of Saint Benedict*, which warns about excessive curiosity, these words of Bernard remind us of the place for learning.

The Spirit teaches not by sharpening curiosity but by inspiring charity. And hence, the Bride, when seeking him whom her heart loves, quite properly does not put her trust in mere human prudence, nor yield to the inane conceits of human curiosity. She asks rather for a kiss, that is she calls upon the Holy Spirit by whom she is simultaneously awarded with the choice repast of knowledge and the seasoning of grace. Two kinds of people therefore may not consider themselves to have been gifted with the kiss. This kiss leaves room neither for ignorance nor for lukewarmness.[22]

In this step of receiving grace to do good, Bernard gives names to the two hands that we kiss. "One I shall call liberality because it gives generously; the other fortitude because it powerfully defends whatever it gives. One who will not be found ungrateful must kiss each of these hands, in order to acknowledge and praise God as the giver and conserver of all good things."[23]

Kissing the two hands, in illumination, one grows in appreciation of God's generosity and strength in preparation for the ultimate relationship of union.

21. Bernard, *Song of Songs I,* 7.
22. Bernard, *Song of Songs I,* 49.
23. Bernard, *Song of Songs I,* 38.

The unitive way permeates Bernard's *On the Song of Songs* and the material invites us to dive deeply into it with reckless abandon. In the book on Bernard in the Classics of Western Spirituality, the author of the introduction to the sermons states that the topics related to the experience of union with God in the sermons will "call to mind and sum up everything discussed so far."[24] Though it may seem rather sweeping to say, his sermons are the sum of his writings and his life. To Bernard, the Song of Songs fully expresses the longings of the soul as the soul contemplates the mystery of God and experiences God's presence.

Keeping with our descriptive metaphor of the three kisses, the unitive way, as the highest goal of union with God, this step of presence, takes us, at long last, to the kiss of his mouth.

> His living, active word is to me a kiss, not indeed an ad-
> hering of the lips that can sometimes belie a union of
> hearts, but an unreserved infusion of joys, a revealing of
> mysteries, a marvelous and indistinguishable mingling
> of the divine light with the enlightened mind, which,
> joined in truth to God, is one spirit with him.[25]

Bernard's words flow as the words of one in love. It is not surprising to learn that sermon 2, from which the quote above is taken, is an Advent sermon. Bernard's longing reveals his heart as one who has waited eagerly for his love, knowing that so many in the Jewish world waited for the incarnation, yet it did not come in their time. He expresses shame that many Christians take the incarnation for granted.

Bernard continues to use the word "experience" frequently and repeats that unitive experience is the culmination of the spiritual journey.

> As we grow in grace and learn to trust in the Lord,
> our experience of love increases until we come to feel
> God's kiss on the mouth. The kiss is an event complete
> and absolute in itself; its unity would be lost were its

24. Leclercq, "Introduction," 46.
25. Bernard, *Song of Songs I*, 8.

elements separated. Thus, Bernard does not analyze the experience, but simply describes it in words such as, "the delights of contemplation lead on to that ecstatic repose that is the fruit of the kiss of his mouth."[26]

These descriptions, found in the sermons of Bernard, reveal a deep intimacy that is beyond analysis and best not attempted. These visits of God are pure gift, sheer grace, and there is nothing one can do to make them happen. The best hope is to be available, willing, full of desire, and eager to know this kiss of his mouth.

Understand that for Bernard this union with God is not a permanent state of the joining of the egos but a fleeting encounter. The joining of the wills may describe it better, as in the Gethsemane prayer of Jesus as he prayed, "Let your will be done" (Matt 26:42). This drink of living water, of union, quenches the thirst as only God can and invites the creature to long for more.

To those who are uncomfortable with this third way, this unitive way, which speaks of personal encounters of ecstasy and delight, take heart! If there is concern that these experiences might be exaggerated or not in keeping with Scripture, consider the source of these sermons. Because Bernard knows and loves Scripture, Scripture references fill up the margins on each page. The references are to the Gospels, the letters of Paul, other wisdom literature, and the prophets. Bernard believed he was in touch with the truer, deeper meaning not only of the Song of Songs, but also of the invitation from God, found throughout Scripture, to come closer, to enjoy the intimacy of union with God.

This intimacy, this unitive way, according to Bernard, is for everyone, not just for the saints and monks.

> He says: "Arise, make haste, my love, my dove, my beautiful one." Happy the conscience which deserves to hear these words! These words are not so applied to the Church as to exclude any one of us, who together are the Church, from a share in its blessings. For in this respect

---

26. Leclercq, "Introduction," 47.

we are all, universally and without distinction, called to possess the blessings as our heritage.[27]

To Bernard, humankind is of immense value to God. And that value lies in God, through union with God, not in ourselves. Our likeness with God is the bond between the bride and the Bridegroom. By God's grace, as sheer gift, God made humankind in God's image, which provides the only hope for union.

Being aware of our sinfulness only enhances our love of God; however, it is common to continue to feel very unworthy, which of course is the truth. We will never be worthy, and that is precisely the point. That truth of being known and loved is what catches our breath, what moves us to tears. While we were yet sinners, Christ died for us (Rom 5:8). He calls us not only to friendship but to intimacy with the Bridegroom. Realization of our unworthiness may be the most common reason, albeit unconscious, for the wide-spread rejection of this notion of union with God. Bernard is quick to encourage all, regardless of how we perceive ourselves, that to all of us God is mystery, beyond our understanding. That, however, should not keep us from seeking him whom our heart loves (Song 3:1). Bernard tells us more about seeking.

> Nor, I think, will a soul cease to seek him even when it has found him. It is not with steps of the feet that God is sought but with the heart's desire; and when the soul happily finds him its desire is not quenched but kindled.[28]

Bernard returns to speaking of "the kiss of his mouth" in sermon 7, still preparing the listeners for his teaching on this supreme kiss. Sermon 8 is no disappointment. He warns the audience at the beginning to "listen with more than usual attention to a theme that is sweet to the spirit above all others."[29]

Throughout the collection we find passages illustrating Bernard's awareness that we are the creatures and God is the Creator. There is a likeness because we are created in God's image, however,

27. Bernard, *Song of Songs III*, 97–98.
28. Bernard, *Song of Songs IV*, 188.
29. Bernard, *Song of Songs I*, 45.

we are finite and limited, while God is not. Though the unitive way is full and glorious and includes ecstasy and delight, the experience of it does not encompass all of who God is.

> But if you love the Lord your God with your whole heart, whole mind, whole strength, and leaping with ardent feeling beyond that love of love with which active love is satisfied and having received the Spirit in fullness, are wholly aflame with that divine love to which the former is a step, then God is indeed experienced, although not as he truly is, a thing impossible for any creature, but rather in relation to your power to enjoy.[30]

Bernard found support for his position not only from his understanding of Scripture, but also from his own experience and from that of his readers. Experience confirms the understanding of the author as well. Since the experience of this unitive way cannot be explained and attempts to fully describe it are found wanting as it is beyond our finite ability to express, it could be of value to provide a few more examples from Bernard.

> It is a slumber which is vital and watchful, which enlightens the heart, drives away death, and communicates eternal life. For it is a genuine sleep that yet does not stupefy the mind but transports it. And, I say it without hesitation, it is a death, for the Apostle Paul in praising people still living in the flesh spoke thus: "For you have died, and your life is hid with Christ in God."[31]

Since the word "contemplation" is currently in vogue and seems to have many definitions depending on the use, it might be helpful to consider Bernard's sense of this word "contemplation" as it applies to the unitive way in his sermons.

> This kind of ecstasy, in my opinion, is alone or principally called contemplation. Not to be gripped during life by material desires is a mark of human virtue; but to gaze without the use of bodily likenesses is the sign

---

30. Bernard, *Song of Songs III*, 35.
31. Casey, *Athirst for God*, 52.

of angelic purity. Each, however, is a divine gift, each is
a going out of oneself, each a transcending of self, but in
one, one goes much farther than in the other. You have
so over-leaped the pleasures of the flesh that you are no
longer responsive to concupiscence even in the least, nor
gripped by its allure.[32]

After many pages describing this union, going around and
around the idea, as he often did on many topics, Bernard then goes
for the heart of it. His nickname, Dr. Mellifluus, meaning "having
a sweet flavor, like honey," comes from this method of preaching.
It is not so much that he wrote sweetly as the name might indicate,
but that he would circle around as a bee circles a flower, looking for
just the right place, and then would go for it. Once he has circled
the material for a while, the listener is more apt to be ready for the
heart, the truth, the sweetness of the message. Here we have one
example of the result of this circling.

> But we think of God and man as dwelling in each other
> in a very different way, because their wills and their sub-
> stances are distinct and different; that is, their substances
> are not intermingled, yet their wills are in agreement;
> and this union is for them a communion of wills and an
> agreement in charity. Happy is this union, but compared
> with the other, it is no union at all.
> Yet man truly abides in God from all eternity, for he
> is loved from all eternity; and God truly abides in man,
> when he is loved by man.[33]

There is no indication that union with God leads to being
equal with God. If anything, it is just the opposite. Again, there is a
mutuality but not equality. Our part, and this only by God's grace,
is to be willing. Christ has shown us how to be opened, how to be
made willing to be obedient (Phil 2:5–11).

> Although she may pour out her whole self in love, what
> is that compared to the inexhaustible fountain of his
> love? The stream of love does not flow equally from her

32. Casey, *Athirst for God*, 54.
33. Bernard, *Song of Songs IV*, 57.

who loves and from him who is love, the Creator and the creature, any more than a thirsty man can be compared to a fountain. Will the desire of [the bride's] heart fail in their purpose because she has not the strength to keep pace with a giant, or rival honey in sweetness, the lamb in gentleness, or the lily in whiteness? No. Although the creature loves less, being a lesser being, yet if it loves with its whole heart nothing is lacking, for it has given all.[34]

The unitive way offers healing in the soul. God does not demand that we do anything other than be available and willing for God to do the work. And God is active, healing the soul, growing the interior fruit of the Spirit, whether one is aware of it or not.

This active healing of the soul by God is a blessing to the person and to God, and also has an even bigger ripple effect in the world. As was mentioned earlier, the Classic Three Ways provides benefits enough on its own, but there is even more. Once we have experienced God active in us, in these ways delightful beyond description, then God calls us and equips us to go out to the world to be part of the healing of a hurting world. This fourth way is the unitive/active way. And it joins the cycle, beginning with our initial awareness and moving through the purgative way, the illuminative way, the unitive way, and then the unitive/active way. Because these words are cumbersome and not familiar, be remined of the more familiar words that go with each way: the way of letting go, seeing with the heart, intimacy, and then lastly, the dance.

Our love relationship with God, affirming God in us, cannot help but move us, with God's love, out to the world to be God's hands and feet. And then when we are out serving in the world, we must continue to be replenished by God and to listen again for whatever God would want of us. Often, we see our need to let go some more.

It is characteristic of true and pure contemplation that when the mind is ardently aglow with God's love, it is sometimes so filled with zeal and the desire to gather to God those who will love him with equal abandon that it

---

34. Bernard, *Song of Songs IV*, 186.

gladly forgoes contemplative leisure for the endeavor of preaching. And then, with its desire at least partially satisfied, it returns to its leisure with an eagerness proportionate to its successful interruption, until, refreshed again with the food of contemplation, it hastens to add to its conquests with renewed strength and experienced zeal.[35]

Much wasted energy doing things in the name of God could be reduced dramatically by first listening for God's leading. Bernard provides some examples of the way of love, which is the most effective way to serve others since God will provide just what we need to do the work God calls us to do. The rest we can lay down for others to pick up if God calls them to it.

You see here a holy man violently tossed between the fruit of action and the quiet of contemplation. For this man the only remedy, the last resort, is prayer and frequent appeal to God that he would deign to show us unceasingly what he wishes us to do, at what time, and in what measure.[36]

We close our study of these sermons of Bernard with an appreciation of his passion for God and God's people and his great love and knowledge of Scripture. Had he lived longer, we can only imagine how many more sermons on the Song of Songs he would have given, for he was on sermon 86 when he died and had reached only the third chapter of the Song of Songs!

What is more important is that we are encouraged to be intentional in loving God. As we believe that we are truly loved and come to see our tremendous need for forgiveness and grace, we respond to God with a willing spirit to learn how to love God in return. Sound too good to be true? Well, it is; yet . . . it is true! That is the paradox of the adventure of faith.

There have been those in high places who agree. In the year 1953, the eight-hundredth anniversary of the death of Bernard of Clairvaux, Pope Pius XII promulgated an encyclical on Bernard's

35. Bernard, *Song of Songs III*, 103.
36. Bernard, *Song of Songs III*, 104.

life and teaching entitled "Doctor Mellifluus: On Saint Bernard of Clairvaux, the Last of the Fathers." In it, Pope Pius XII goes to great length to say that reading Bernard could help solve the problems of the world today.

> Wherefore, since love for God is gradually growing cold today in the hearts of many, or is even completely quenched, we feel that these writings of the "Doctor Mellifluus" should be carefully pondered; because from their content, which in fact is taken from the Gospels, a new and heavenly strength can flow both into individual and on into social life, to give moral guidance, bring it into line with Christian precepts, and thus be able to provide timely remedies for the many grave ills which afflict mankind. For when men do not have the proper love for their Creator, from Whom comes everything they have when they do not love one another, then, as often happens, they are separated from one another by hatred and deceit, and so quarrel bitterly among themselves. Now God is the most loving Father of us all, and we are all brethren in Christ, we whom He redeemed by shedding His precious Blood. Hence, as often as we fail to return God's love or to recognize His divine fatherhood with all due reverence the bonds of brotherly love are unfortunately shattered and as, alas, is so often evident, discord, strife and enmity unhappily are the result, so much so as to undermine and destroy the very foundations of human society.[37]

Is it any wonder that loving God with all of who we are is the first and greatest commandment? This teaching of Jesus is central to what it means to be a Christian, a Christ-one, and the benefit is not just for us, but for the entire world. It is not the easy way. Loving God with all of who we are will take us from awakening to God's love through the purgative way, the illuminative way, the unitive way, and the unitive/active way. There will be times when we want to quit. However, by God's grace, the desire to quench our thirst keeps us on the journey. Our only hope is found in the truth

---

37. Pius, "Doctor Mellifluus," 4.

that this highest invitation is available and possible, not just for saints, but for everyone.

This teaching that seemed relevant to help solve the world's problems in 1953 appears to be just as important today in a world that is spinning out of control and in which we rarely hear of love for God. Bernard saw loving God as the best hope for the world and lived it himself. Perhaps we could learn something from him. Imagine one person at a time moving into that graced space of first knowing of God's love, then learning to love God and God's people in return. It may be our best hope for world peace, one person at a time.

Reflection with Bernard

Settle In

Take a few moments to settle in. Look around. Listen. Notice what you notice. Feel the chair supporting you and your feet on the floor. Get comfortable. Stretch a bit if that helps. Take a deep breath or two to let your body help your mind slow down. Be aware of God's face turned toward you in love, right here, now. *Behold God beholding you in love.* When you are settled in, move to the options below.

1. Enjoy this writing by Bernard—just soak in it; immerse yourself in it.

"On Loving God"
Four Degrees of Love
as We Mature in Faith:

Love self for self's sake
Love God for self's sake
Love God for God's sake
Love self for God's sake

Ask God to help you see times when you live in each degree. Bernard says not many people get to the last degree, to see ourselves as God sees us. To live more in the space of loving God for God's sake, loving the giver not just the gift, is a call to us all.

2. What hopes are awakened in you as you ponder your love relationship with God increasing so that it overflows to a thirsty world?

3. The Scripture passage, "It is no longer I who live, but Christ who lives in me" (Gal 2:20) refers to our being willing to be crucified with Christ, to die to self. Spend a little time pondering what that looks like in your own life.

4. Describe your readiness and eagerness to receive from God in your emptiness. What invitation or offering do you hear?

5. Rest in God, without words, opening yourself to whatever God has for you.

6. Close with gratitude if it is true for you.

5

The Classic Three Ways Plus One as Found in *The Dialogue* by Catherine of Siena

CATHERINE OF SIENA LIVED fully each of the Classic Three Ways Plus One. Born in the Fontebranda district of Siena, Italy, March 25, 1347, the twenty-fourth of twenty-five children, Caterina di Giacomo di Benincasa was headstrong and independent, even in her youth. It is difficult to be certain about many details of her life because over the years they have been woven through with pious legend. What we do know is that her father was a wool-dyer and made a good living in an area that was rife with class conflict and revolution.

Legend has it that Catherine felt called to follow an austere life after a vision given to her when she was six years old. In the vision Christ appeared to her seated on an imperial throne dressed in papal attire with a tiara on his head. In the company of the apostles Peter, Paul, and John, Christ smiled lovingly on her with eyes full of majesty, raised his right hand over her, and made the sign of the cross to give her a priestly blessing. The next year, Catherine made a private vow of virginity. She was fifteen when she cut off her hair in defiance of efforts to make her marry. Because there was no privacy in her home, Catherine retreated to the secret cell of her mind, discovering the cell of self-knowledge. This cell was to become an immense interior spiritual life. Her parents, disappointed with her direction in life since they wanted the dowry as financial help, made her the scullery maid for the family. Surprisingly to them, Catherine loved the work of serving her siblings, nieces, and nephews. Finally, at her father's insistence the family ceased to interfere, and she was granted privacy for prayerful solitude.

There was a local Dominican third order of laywomen, called the Mantellate, where Catherine made private promises of poverty, chastity, and obedience. She was eighteen when she received the Dominican habit and began three years of solitude and prayer, going out only for daily Mass at San Domenico, a hub of Dominican teaching. During these formative years she learned to read. She gained a reputation of great holiness and purification through asceticism and experienced ecstasies and spiritual struggles that culminated when she was twenty in her "mystical marriage with Christ."[1] It was a strong encounter in which she knew Christ was pleased with her prayerful devotion and did not want that to stop, but at the same time was propelling her into the world to serve her neighbor out of love for God.

These social work years were full of the warmly human side of Catherine as she looked out for the destitute, much like our current day Mother Teresa, and served as a nurse in homes and hospitals. However, during this full time she never gave up her contemplative life and often could be found in her room, teaching others about the Bible, theology, and God's grace and truth.

These years gave her some notoriety as people were drawn to spend time with her to learn of her spiritual wisdom, which also taught her about conflict and criticism in the form of opposition from friars and the Mantellate. Her fame and her travel outside of Siena were of concern to them.

Her mystical experiences continued to increase and intensify. She had a climactic point in her mystical death, symbolic of union with God, in 1370 when she was 23. Her body lay seemingly lifeless for four hours and those around her discerned that she was dead. This experience prompted her with a clearer vision that she was to introduce God's truth to the world. It was after her mystical death

---

1. King, *Christian Mystics*, 85.

that she began writing letters to share God's truth. She encouraged clergy reform and a greater dedication to the church.

Another epidemic of the Black Death broke out in Siena, so Catherine and her followers tended the sick and dying. During this time, she received the stigmata, though by her request the wounds were not made visible.

Political tensions were mounting in Siena, as in all of Italy, and Catherine found herself called to intervene in prayer and in council wherever she saw God's truth being compromised. She worked tirelessly in political and religious affairs. She was greatly concerned for the church. She played an active part in the ecclesiastical politics as she traveled to Avignon to visit Pope Gregory XI to plead with him to return to Rome. Her argument was that care for spiritual things was above temporal things. Though the Western/Papal Schism did occur regardless of her efforts, she went to Florence as peace mediator, at the request of Pope Gregory XI. Historians indicate she was used as a pawn often by the political leaders of the day, but she served faithfully as one sent by God. There is much more that has been written about her involvement, too much to include here, but for our purposes we must emphasize that she was fully engaged, however God led her. One favorite book about Catherine is titled *My Nature Is Fire*, indicating her fervor, energy, and devotion.

When Catherine was thirty, she began her major work, *The Dialogue*, and continued working on it during this time of unrest. During this same time until her death at thirty-three, she directed a household in the old fortress of Belcaro, outside of Siena, where women and men lived by strict observance to poverty and alms. She was greatly exhausted by her public life and the sacrifices she had made. Her final years were filled with physical agony due to her strict asceticism, thus she realized and began to teach that such strictness was not necessary. She died on April 29, 1380. That day is now recognized as her feast day. In 1461, shortly after her death, she was recognized as a saint and in 1939 was declared the patron saint of Italy. In 1970 she was proclaimed a Doctor of the Church, along with Teresa of Avila, the first women to be given this title. Currently, of the thirty-six Doctors of the Church today, four are women: these two along with Hildegard of Bingen and Therese of Lisieux.

Some say that Catherine composed and dictated much of *The Dialogue* within a state of ecstasy and that she completed it in five days. However, most believe that it took her about a year to complete it. In her book, she expressed many of her concerns about church unity, personal austerity, and devotion, love of neighbor, clergy reform, God's grace and mercy, and the passionate search for God's truth. One version of this classic work is titled *Little Talks with God* (see bibliography) and has made her teachings more available to a wider audience. The main point of the book is to provide spiritual seekers a guidebook for incorporating the spiritual in the everyday, as Catherine did. She wrote (dictated) in the language of the people and so it was written, rather than in the Latin of the church. She had a devoted and large following among all classes of society in Siena. Catherine's "little talks" help us live our own quest for God's love and truth within our busy lives.

There are other sources that reveal Catherine's inner life, primarily her almost four hundred letters that remain today, with applications of spiritual teachings. She also recorded a collection of twenty-six prayers, most of them in the time just prior to her death. In them we have access to her concept of divinity. But *The Dialogue* is the mature fruit of her spiritual teachings. All together they provide a rich insight into Catherine's personality, activities, and inner journey. Our focus will be on *The Dialogue*, just to limit the scope, as we look for her love for God and the Classic Three Ways Plus One. This descriptive process looms front and center throughout.

Her value of interior wholeness, internal unity, opens the door to mystical and contemplative union, as recognized by both the East and the West today. Catherine taught that all can achieve the connective harmony leading to union with God at whatever pace or intensity they choose and in whatever life circumstances they find themselves. Therefore her spirituality is relevant to every age.

Catherine called *The Dialogue* "my book" as she entrusted it in a letter to Raymond of Capua, a trusted friend and confessor. The framework for the book is four questions that the soul (herself) asks of God. She always referred to herself as the soul. Then God replied to the soul, revealing much useful truth. The pattern followed is her petition, God's response, and then her thanksgiving.

> Her four questions are: for herself (later specified in a plea that she be allowed to suffer in atonement for sin); for the reform of the Church; for the whole world, and especially for peace in relation to rebellious Christians; for divine providence in all things, but specifically in regard to "a certain case that had arisen."[2]

At the outset, before the first way, the purgative, the way of letting go, we hear God say to Catherine that to make the journey the soul must be thirsty! One does not make the journey if one is not thirsty; the thirst is the motivation and is essential. This correlates to the awakening to a longing for God in our diagram. God also strongly encourages that the soul not go alone. "If two or three or more are gathered in my name, there am I in the midst of them" (Matt 18:20). Spiritual direction was in full bloom during these years, and souls were encouraged to walk this faith journey with a spiritual director.

Prior to her experience of the purgative way, Catherine's vibrant and life-changing awakening to God's love when merely a child led her to the humbling path of self-knowledge, introducing her to the awareness of her need to choose to love God. She realized that it took courage and that the choice would result in losses, even as it anchored her more deeply in God. She endured a withdrawal into spiritual life for three years as she devoted herself to prayer. This time can be seen as a purgative time, a letting go, an emptying by God's hand.

The central part of the book is an image God gave her of a bridge, an image of Christ's body being the bridge between the soul and God. Those who choose to pass under the bridge do not make it to God. At times she refers to the bridge as a tree. If the soul indicates that it cannot climb this tree because it is too high,

2. Catherine, *The Dialogue*, 16.

God answers her by showing her the hollowed-out stairs in his very body, so she can make the journey. This image is referenced and expanded throughout the book. The first stair is clearly indicative of the purgative way, as it is the feet of Christ. Christ has made a staircase of his body for us. Christ's nailed feet, like the root of a tree, provide the anchor for us and are nourished in the soil of humility, the greatest ingredient on the path of virtue. They require the giving up of the self-will so that one develops a deep and genuine humility. It is called the imperfect state and is a place for self-knowledge. The theme of self-knowledge is repeated as essential for moving on the journey of faith. If we don't know that we need God, that we are sinners in need of a redeemer, we can be tempted to take the idea of a journey of faith rather casually. Catherine's self-knowledge resulted in her humility, which in turn gave her a strong desire, often experienced by those who knew her as a fire within her.

As Catherine climbs the symbolic stairs in Christ's body, she comments that in these three stairs there are three spiritual stages. Continuing with the first step, the feet of Christ are a refuge for the beginner. When Catherine steps onto the feet of Christ, she is aware that her love is for pleasure and self-advantage. On this step the soul becomes aware of the memory of grave sin and then understands the punishment that it deserves. The will then hates the sin and is undone by it. Also on this step is the awareness of the love Christ bears for the soul, and the soul climbs on in love with "the feet of their affection stripped of slavish fear."[3] In this way the soul becomes faithful rather than faithless, serving out of love rather than fear. It yearns for the root of selfish love to be dug up.

She goes on to say that many take this step out of fear and weariness, but she discerns "that the first ordinary step must be climbed with both feet, that is, with affection and desire."[4] There is a change taking place within her as she realizes she is not alone nor dependent solely on her own effort. The turning point is as

3. Catherine, *The Dialogue*, 113.
4. Meade, *My Nature*, 110.

she begins to learn to rely on God's mercy. She encourages us with these words.

> However, if they persevere and take advantage of the light of discernment, they may begin to progress to love of virtue. At the first stair, love must become strong enough to cast out fear and overcome weariness; this is the area where change must take place because love is essential to growth in virtue.[5]

Only as she is emptied, hollowed out, is there space for her to receive new wisdom. With the light, we are encouraged on this journey to move to the illuminative way.

There are many references to light and how God illumines Catherine's thinking. It is more than a way of thinking, however; it is a way of being. The heart is changed and made tender. She says, "Only hearts as hard as diamonds could fail to be softened by such measureless love."[6]

As Catherine continues moving along the bridge that is the body of Christ, creating a stairway for the journey of faith, the fruit of the first step, tremendous desire and unquenchable thirst, propel her onward. Her love of virtue and the importance of giving her will to God move her to choose to love as God loves. The symbol of the second stair is Christ's open, wounded heart, full of love for all, but particularly for the individual making the journey at that time. It is like a shop filled with fragrant spices and a warm-hearted love for all. To continue with the tree image, the open heart of Christ is like the interior marrow of the tree. It is infused wisdom including a willingness to suffer with Christ. This awareness, however, prompts her to see her own sinfulness, as she had a high opinion of herself and received great pleasure in her own sacrifice. In this new light, Catherine is more aware of her own fragility and turns to God in humble repentance to learn how to love well. Now her love is no longer full of herself but of the

5. Meade, *My Nature*, 110.
6. Meade, *My Nature*, 111.

passion of Christ. She sees that suffering purifies and transforms her spirit as she opens to God's work in her.

Catherine's book uses an imagery not used by our other heroes of the faith. In the illuminative way, seeing with the heart, the relationship with God is called a friendship with mutual love. It is a good thing on the way to union. There is a love in friendship that is based on God's mercy and is not ruled by fear—thus it is progress from the purgative way. After his resurrection, Christ told his disciples that he must go away and then return. In the same way along our journey of faith, God withdraws loving feelings and the comfort that the soul has known. God does not withdraw grace, just the feelings. That is crucial to understand. Grace is not withdrawn. During this time the soul has the chance to respond to God's withdrawing of feelings and comforts. If the soul does not turn back but perseveres in humility, not demanding or complaining, waiting with humble patience and hope, she will learn what God is wanting to teach her. She will see that she was loving the gifts more than the giver, that her love for God was truly more out of self-interest. At that point she can come back to seek God in truth, and God will return the feelings and comfort in God's time, whenever it is helpful and not harmful.

This new place of light and wisdom leads her to acknowledge God's providence in her life, in the good and the bad, trusting God is in it all. Catherine begins to love with Christ's love in her, loving what God loves. It is clearly pointed out to her that one cannot climb only one stair. Once one begins the journey all three stairs must be climbed; it is just the way of God. Catherine becomes eager to move on to the third stair.

The symbol for the third stair in the body of Christ is his mouth. It is a symbol overflowing with meaning for Catherine as she likens it to the liturgical kiss of peace and finds a deep peace because her will is dead. She first experienced calm, then tasted the peace of obedience, knowing she was finally in the space where God wanted her.

Soon after moving to the third step and encountering the mouth of Christ, Catherine moves to serving her neighbor. To her it appears they are one and the same. While all the heroes of faith in these pages lived lives full of service to God and God's people, Catherine spends little time in *The Dialogue* describing the unitive way, though it is apparent in her life. Her writing/dictating occurred in this unitive place. At times it seems she is already moving there in the illuminative way. It's not a problem for the lines between the Three Classic Ways Plus One to blur at times. Of course, we must acknowledge again that God can surprise us, woo us, and bring us to deeper faith any way that suits. Our little schema is not prescriptive but rather is descriptive of how growth in faith usually happens, and thus it is beneficial to know.

This unitive/active way is prevalent throughout Catherine's life, and we will make a point of her devotion. *The Dialogue* even provides a description of the water illustration given in chapter 2 that defines and describes the Classic Three Ways Plus One. God suggests that Catherine, and other souls of course, continue to drink from the living fountain while serving—instead of leaving the fountain to serve. My systematic theology professor, Dr. Merwyn Johnson, once asked the class this question: "Is prayer a work or is work a prayer?" Perhaps this question comes close to reflecting the life of Catherine as she served God's people while still staying fully connected to God in love and prayer. "Prayerfully dependent" is a phrase used by Grace Church in Greenville, South Carolina, encouraging dependency on God momently, with a willingness, even a strong desire, to move as God leads, knowing we cannot do it on our own.

As the soul moves through the three stairs and finally crosses the bridge, she is very thirsty for the living water. In the Gospel of John, Jesus speaks with the Samaritan woman and tells her, "The water I will give will become in them a spring of water gushing up into eternal life" (John 4:14). Our thirst is not a bad thing. In a sermon at Grace Church, Scofield Foster, one of the ministers, said that our thirst is good, even though it may lead us to try to quench the thirst with things other than the living water of Christ. We turn to shallow cisterns, such as prestige, wealth, or human relationships, thinking that they will quench the thirst. They don't, and we are tempted to blame the thirst. But Foster reminded us that our thirst is good. We are brought back to Augustine's famous prayer, "You have made us for yourself and our hearts are restless until they rest in you."[7]

God also says never to stop offering the incense of fragrant prayers for the salvation of souls. God calls us to participate in this process, and our prayer is an integral part. The rest of Catherine's life was spent in ardent prayer and service to bring souls to God. Keeping the giver in mind when receiving gifts can be helped by being aware of Christ who is the joining of the divine and human nature. We cannot look at him without being aware of both the gift and giver. God gives her this wisdom.

Many more examples of the unitive/active way are available to us throughout Catherine's life, but there is something rather unique in her understanding. She was so very present to God and listening in her prayer, that she learned much from asking questions.

Her understanding may be more available to the reader in the version of *The Dialogue* called *Little Talks with God*. In it, the divisions of the conversation are "On Divine Mercy," "On Discretion," "On Prayer," and "On Obedience." It is the same material, but perhaps more focused and easier to grasp. The last section, "On Obedience," relates to this "Plus One" way, this fourth way. In it, God speaks of where obedience may be found, what destroys it, what are the signs of one possessing it, and what supports or nourishes it.

As we begin to delve into obedience, look again at our diagram of the Classic Three Ways Plus One. Notice that lower right corner, where one who is serving well in that unitive/active place can become tired, unsatisfied, and even burned out. Sadly, this seems to be rather common in ministry, for both clergy and laity. Catherine hears from God with such clarity about what causes this that it is worth noting.

Let's begin with how well it is going first. The concept of John 17 is alive and well, as Catherine prays,

7. Augustine, *Confessions*, 2.

I do not beseech you for myself alone, Father, but for
the whole world, and particularly for the mystical body
of the holy church that this truth given to me, miserable
one that I am, by you, eternal truth, may shine in your
ministers.

Also, I beseech you especially for all those whom
you have given me, and whom you have made one with
me, and whom I love with a particular love.[8]

Earlier on in the same page she asked God to grant her prayer
because without God nothing is done, as stated clearly in John
15:5. So all is going well in this unitive/active way, the overflow of
ministry coming from this mutual love relationship between the
minister and God. One way it is described in Catherine's prayer
is, "Cause your holy church to bloom with the fragrant flowers of
good and holy pastors, who by their sweet odor shall extinguish
the stench of the putrid flowers of sin."[9]

God reveals that obedience is found in Christ and that we
should look at his life. God also responds that what destroys obedience is pride, produced by self-love and desire to please others.
In my experience of over twenty-five years of spiritual direction, I
can vouch for that. The desire is usually to please the congregation
or the groups one serves. It is not easy to catch at first because it
seems wrapped up in good ministry. But when pleasing the people
takes precedence over pleasing God, it is unhealthy and detrimen-
tal to the server and those served.

One sign of being obedient is patience. Christ was patient
realizing that his life really wasn't about him. Conversely when
we are aware of being impatient, we can suspect that we have lost
our obedience. We are called not to place our love in finite things
but only in God. It is suggested that we keep the key of obedience
tied fast on a cord around our waist. The word for the cord in this
translation is "self-contempt." This phrase was used often in the
time when Catherine lived, but it does not sit well with our current
awareness of shame and the damage it causes. With psychology's

8. Catherine, *Little Talks*, 108.
9. Catherine, *Little Talks*, 116.

influence today we know about healthy self-love versus unhealthy. I prefer using the phrases self-centeredness, self-interest, or selfish desires, and I encourage people to move toward a willingness to die to self, by God's grace. Again, Catherine exhorts us, all ministers, to become self-aware, to be intentional to know ourselves. We will catch our self-centeredness sooner if we are spending time paying attention to what God is wanting to show us. Humility leads to obedience—a willingness to die to self—and pride leads to disobedience. So, we ask, what are we to do once we see our failure, once we see the signs?

Catherine's dialogue with God is clear as God says that whatever we need is found in sweet Christ Jesus. He is the epitome of patience and offers it to us all. As the vine with the branches, we are one. In him we find obedience. We must keep this key of obedience in our hand and "fasten it to the love of pleasing me, your Creator."[10] We must not take our delight in the praise of people.

> Such as these are apt to lose their key. For if they suffer
> a little extra fatigue, or mental or bodily tribulations and
> if, as often happens, the hand of holy desire loosens its
> grasp, they will lose it. And what will prove to them that
> they have lost it? Impatience, for patience was united to
> obedience, and their impatience proves that obedience
> does not dwell in their soul.[11]

So, again, what are we to do? As shown in the diagram, we want to return to that dependence on God, so perhaps we are to return to the purgative way, the way of letting go, of holding lightly. Questions we might want to ask are, "What am I grasping too tightly? Where have I moved away from prayerful dependence on God and moved toward my own prideful way that longs to please the crowd rather than God?" I let go as God leads, making my way around the circle with a deepening awareness of Christ and of myself each time. God helps me loosen my grasp to empty me of whatever I'm holding onto too tightly. Then there is space for some new light, some filling, some deeper wisdom, and that

10. Catherine, *Little Talks*, 125.
11. Catherine, *Little Talks*, 126.

moves me toward the place of union again. The union may not have been totally gone, but it was unavailable. From this beautiful place of intimate union, I move again into the dance that has all the energy, all the resources needed for the unitive/active work to which we are invited by God.

God's conversation continues with descriptions of the life lived with obedience still in hand. God uses words such as peace, rest, forgiveness, stripped of worldly desire, without fatigue, cheerful, hearty joy, generosity, and liberty, all covered by love, by God's grace in Christ Jesus.

Catherine closes the book with a summary and then a prayer. Here is part of the prayer.

> For I have tasted and seen with your light, the abyss of you, the eternal Trinity.
>
> You have been willing to condescend to my need and to that of your creatures, the need to examine the thoughts and feelings of our hearts. Having first given me the grace to ask the question, you reply to it, and satisfy your servant, penetrating me with a ray of grace, so that in that light, I may give you thanks.
>
> Clothe me, clothe me with yourself, eternal Truth, so that I may run my mortal course with true obedience and the light of holy faith.[12]

Reflection with Catherine

Settle In

Take a few moments to settle in. Look around. Listen. Notice what you notice. Feel the chair supporting you and your feet on the floor. Get comfortable; stretch a bit if that helps. Take a deep breath or two to let your body help your mind slow down. Be aware of God's face turned toward you in love, right here, now. *Behold God beholding you in love.* When you are settled in, move to the options below. Select whichever ones speak to you.

12. Catherine, *Little Talks*, 141.

1. While her purgative times were ample, most seemed her own idea. She was convicted of the need to discipline herself. She agreed that much of it was not healthy, but of course there is a middle ground. What do you see as a healthy middle ground for discipline?

2. Catherine relates much about illuminative times as she was being taught. How were her "aha" moments like some of the moments you've had—moving you toward union?

3. As you were reading about obedience, where were you convicted? What temptations in your life connect with the temptations in the conversation she had with God?

4. Over your time in ministry, what have you learned to help you avoid this pitfall? How quickly do you catch that you've moved away? How do you see this invitation back to the purgative way as a possible help?

5. Spend some time with her prayer. Where does it speak to you? Which phrases resonate?

6. Rest in God without words, opening yourself to whatever God has for you.

7. If it is true, close your reflection time with gratitude for who God is and for what God has done, is doing, and will do.

6

The Classic Three Ways Plus One as Found in *The Spiritual Exercises* of Ignatius of Loyola

MANY OTHER ROMAN CATHOLICS were aware of the need for reform at the time Luther posted his Ninety-five Theses to the Wittenberg door, and as Calvin was writing his *Institutes*. Protestants often call it the Counter Reformation, while it is more commonly known as the Roman Catholic Reform by those within the Roman Catholic Church. Two individuals come to mind most quickly when speaking of reform from within: Ignatius of Loyola and Teresa of Avila, two sixteenth-century Spanish mystics. Neither of them had easy roads on their faith journeys, and it is interesting to note that they are both considered to be "pilgrims." Ignatius, founder of the Jesuits—the Society of Jesus—in 1540, referred to himself as a pilgrim, such that his autobiography was called *A Pilgrim's Journey*. And *Spiritual Pilgrims: Carl Jung and Teresa of Avila*, a book by John Welch, a contemporary Carmelite, is about Christian individuation, the movement into the wholeness of one's personality as awareness of the union with God deepens. He writes of the spiritual journey of believers, and his main source is *The Interior Castle* by Teresa of Avila.

Ignatius (1491–1556) was born before Teresa (1515–1582), and though they were both in Spain and the years of their lives overlapped, we have no evidence that they ever met. In her writings, however, Teresa tells of the great help she received from the Jesuits as spiritual directors when the Jesuits founded a college in Avila in 1554. She also mentions Ignatius by name in the fifth mansion of *The Interior Castle*, saying, "How many more he [Satan] loses even now, through Father Ignatius (Loyola) who founded the Company (of Jesus)!"[1] It is easy to see the influence of the Jesuits on Teresa in her writings, as many of her central concepts for reform of the Carmelite order are phrased similarly to the words of the Jesuits. We will look at *The Spiritual Exercises* by Ignatius first as well as an introduction to his life, and then in chapter 8 at *The Interior Castle* by Teresa along with a brief biographical sketch of her.

Ignatius was named Inigo Lopez de Loyola in the castle of the Loyola family in the Basque region of Spain. He was the youngest of thirteen children of a family of minor nobility. He grew up with a desire for fame and a love for the military. He entered the military as a young man and was known to be fearless. His life changed dramatically, however, when, during the Battle of Pamplona in 1521, at the age of thirty, a cannonball fractured his left leg in many places. The injury required several surgeries in a time before anesthesia. He was quite vain about his appearance, so was disappointed that he would always walk with a limp.

His recovery time in the hospital, however, proved to be of God. The books that were available to him were about the lives of the saints. He also had some books of chivalry and romance. The story goes that when he would read the stories of romance and chivalry, he would enjoy these books, but the joy was not lasting. In contrast, when he read the stories of the saints, the joy would linger, and it was accompanied by peace. The book that had the greatest influences on his life was *The Life of Christ* by Ludolph of Saxony. In it the author encouraged the reader to use one's imagination to place oneself in the scene in the gospel narrative, paying attention to Jesus and others, and all the senses: sights, smells, sounds, etc. This imaginative process will be explained in greater detail later.

Ignatius decided to leave the life he had lived in order to imitate the saints, especially Dominic, Catherine of Siena, and

---

1. Teresa, *Interior Castle*, 150.

Francis. He developed an intense desire for Christ and to live for him and his purposes. His original plan was to make a pilgrimage to Jerusalem. He went first to the shrine of the black virgin at Monserrat. There he left his fine clothes, as knights used to do when they entered military service. Ignatius put on a pilgrim's tunic and left there for what was intended to be a brief stop at Manresa. He ended up spending almost a year there praying in a cave about seven hours a day, formulating the spiritual exercises. It was a time of great interior development as he struggled with scruples and was given divine illuminations. It was for him the greatest preparation for his life of service.

It is difficult to set a date for the creation of *The Spiritual Exercises* by Ignatius because he first wrote them while in the cave in Manresa from March 1522 to February 1523 as they were given to him by God for his own experience. He continued to refine them and began giving them to his followers. In 1537, at La Storta, he had a deepening of his faith, so much so that it has been called a second Manresa. He and some of his followers had spent forty days in prayer and penance in Venice and had many spiritual visions and consolations. It was there that Ignatius perceived himself intimately united to Jesus and decided to create an order devoted to him and bearing his name. It is an indication of the humility of Ignatius that many other orders were named after their founder, yet Ignatius wanted this new order to bear the name of Jesus, not himself. "Its members should be intimately united to Jesus in prayer and enrolled under the banner of the cross, to ply in a corporate manner his work for the service and glory of God and the welfare of their fellow men and women."[2]

The interior life of Ignatius continued to be the driving force for the Society of Jesus, as he frequently experienced images of the Trinity and contemplated them with delight. His own interior life prompted him to be aware of the great need for discernment, for himself, for his followers, and for any who would serve Christ.

At the beginning of *The Spiritual Exercises*, after various notes to the directors and others, Ignatius states the purpose of

2. Ignatius, *Selected Works*, 42.

the exercises: "To order one's life toward God, without coming to a decision from some disordered attachment pleasing more to self than to God, even if this requires the conquering of self necessary when selfish urges would impede this goal."[3] Right after that is the "Principle and Foundation," a one-page document that presents the logic that is at work throughout the exercises. It begins with the fact that God loves us and that everything in life is given to us so that we might more easily know God and more readily love God in return. So, in our everyday life we are to avoid becoming attached to anything. "Our only desire and our one choice should be this: I want and I choose what better leads to God's deepening of [God's] life in me."[4] Decisions are to be based on whatever is more conducive to the end of greater praise and glory to God. An indifference to wealth or poverty, health or sickness, long life or short life, good reputation or bad reputation was at the heart of this invitation. The retreatant is encouraged to be "indifferent" or undecided until clear, sound reasons for choice appear.

To clarify the name "*The Spiritual Exercises*," we can look at annotation 2 within the exercises:

> For, just as taking a walk, traveling on foot and running are physical exercises, so is the name of spiritual exercises given to any means of preparing and disposing the soul to rid itself of all its disordered affections and then after their removal, of seeking and finding God's will in the ordering of our life for the salvation of our soul.[5]

The Spiritual Exercises is not a treatise on the spiritual life, but rather a detailed description of experiences, a manual if you will, written for spiritual directors who serve as guides for retreatants over a period of thirty days or more.

To grasp a sense of the exercises themselves, the process is as follows. The director assigns Scripture and encourages the retreatant to take about thirty to forty minutes with each passage,

3. Ignatius, *The Spiritual Exercises* (trans. Ganss), 51.

4. Fleming, "Principle and Foundation," 9.

5. Ignatius, *The Spiritual Exercises* (trans. Ganss), 21.

moving into the story, using the imagination, seeing the sights, hearing the sounds, and entering the dialogue as led. The format usually includes a settling-in time before reading the passage with words such as "Behold God, beholding you in love." Next, the retreatant is to read the Scripture for content, reminding oneself of the story. Note here that this imaginative practice comes easily for some but not for others. For those of us who struggle to stay with the story, journaling is a great help. Writing what is happening in the story, with all the details as they come, can keep the focus for the time of prayer on the Scripture.

One example in the second week would be to picture oneself at the birth of Jesus, in the stable outside the inn where there was no room. The retreatant could be anyone in the story, perhaps the daughter of the innkeeper sent out to bring towels and to see if everyone was all right. The retreatant may be encouraged to see Mary holding Jesus, to hear her sing to him, to feel the warmth of the fire Joseph lit, and perhaps even to be asked to hold baby Jesus while Mary naps. Each retreatant experiences it a little differently, often with profoundly deep results. The director listens for the movement of the Holy Spirit in the retreatant and discerns if he or she is ready to move on or would benefit more from remaining with the scene for a repetition, which is more accurately labeled as going deeper into whatever emotions were present during the previous time. Here is one brief example of how entering the Scripture in the imagination can bring healing and growth.

One elderly woman retreatant was sad that she had not married and thus did not have any children; yet holding Jesus that day in her imagination, she felt Mary's comfort and friendship. Mary shared with her that there are not only joys of having children, but that there can also be deep sadness, if the child's life is cut short as was the life of Jesus or if there are other difficulties, even a strained relationship. The woman was more reconciled with her situation and therefore became more involved in the nursery at her church when she returned home; she held the babies and prayed for them as she rocked them.

After the time of prayer is completed, the retreatant is invited to move into a time of paying attention to what happened during that time of prayer. It is not a time to judge the prayer, but simply to notice what were the affects, the feelings, involved and what spoke to the heart. This time is for writing about the prayer time with the intent of sharing what was written with your spiritual director the next day when you meet. Doing this for each of the three to five passages of Scripture provides the content for the daily meeting with the director.

The exercises are divided up into four weeks, however, the weeks do not contain the usual seven days each. They can be viewed more as divisions within the exercises, each with specific intentions. A gifted spiritual director listens for the movement of the Holy Spirit to know when to move on to the next week, or more specifically the next exercise. To begin, the retreatant is encouraged to enter the process with great generosity and courage.

The first week is for removing the disordered affections, with exercises characteristic of the purgative way. The director listens especially for an increased awareness of God's love and mercy in the retreatant. This awareness is the key to moving on. One director and trainer at the Jesuit Center for Spiritual Growth in Wernersville, Pennsylvania, mentioned that for one retreatant, he stayed in the first week for nineteen days because the retreatant had not yet grasped God's infinite love and mercy as a personal encounter. Ignatius was aware of this possibility and covered it in annotation 18, saying that for some people, the first week is all they can do.

Once the retreatant has grasped God's immense love, then that person is ready to move on to the second week. The second week is focused on the life of Jesus up to his triumphal entrance into Jerusalem, with exercises characteristic of the illuminative way. The heart of Ignatian spirituality is the spiritual exercises; the heart of the exercises is the second week; the heart of the second week is discernment, making a choice, so it is essential to spend more time understanding the role of discernment in this week.

The second week begins with a contemplation on the call of Christ to participate with him in spreading his kingdom. It is followed by using the imagination to enter the scenes of the annunciation, incarnation, nativity, and hidden life of Christ. Next are the stories of the public life of Jesus, such as his staying behind in the temple, his reading from the scroll in the temple, his baptism, his temptation in the wilderness, his healing of the blind, lame, etc. The retreatant asks for this grace at the beginning of these Scripture passages: "To gain an interior knowledge of our Lord, who has become man for me, that I may love him more and follow him more closely."[6] These words are often credited to Ignatius, but study has revealed that they were first said by Richard of Chichester (d. 1253), "To know thee more clearly, love thee more dearly, and follow thee more nearly." These words were made familiar to many in the song "Day by Day" from the musical "Godspell."

The retreatant is also invited to contemplate the core values from the "Principle and Foundation," such as indifference, especially related to deciding about a state of life. There are three powerful meditations used, but for this purpose the first one will be discussed in more detail. The second, on the three classes of persons, and the third, on three ways of being humble, will not be addressed as thoroughly here but all are worth investigating. The first is the meditation on the two standards, one of Christ and the other of Lucifer. The retreatant is invited to picture a large battlefield, with Lucifer, the mortal enemy of our human nature, seated on a throne of fire and smoke, horrible and terrifying with his army in Babylon and their standard flying high. The retreatant is asked to listen to what Lucifer says and to notice what means he employs in his effort to reach the whole world. Lucifer admonishes his devils to set up snares and chains, to tempt people to covet riches, so that they may more easily come to vain honor and finally to surging pride. In this order the enemy entices them to other vices.

On the other side of this battlefield is the Lord Christ, our supreme commander and Lord with his army in Jerusalem, lowly, beautiful, and attractive, with their standard flying high. The retreatant is asked to consider Christ as he chooses so many persons to go throughout the world spreading his doctrine. Hear his address

6. Ignatius, *The Spiritual Exercises* (trans. Ganss),148.

as he recommends that they endeavor to aid all persons by attracting them first to the highest degree of spiritual poverty (in opposition to riches); second to reproaches and contempt (in opposition to honor from the world); and third to humility (in opposition to pride). From this they can induce people to all the other virtues.

The choice becomes clear, because the retreatant has already experienced the deep love of God and already desires to return that love in great measure. Choosing whom to serve is a foundational point for the retreatant whether making a life decision or not. All the contemplations that help with discernment in making a good decision are applicable for those making other decisions that occur in life. For some it is more about the renewal of life, and a good director will adjust the exercises to fit the retreatant.

There are rules for the discernment of spirits set up for the first week, and then more rules that are suitable for the second week, as they probe more deeply. One more illustration of discernment will highlight its importance to Ignatius. Discernment of spirits, of consolation and desolation, is helpful daily. He encourages all his followers, then and now, to be sensitive to whether the inner promptings are of the Spirit of God or from a spirit of evil and darkness. He reminds us that it is not always easy to tell the difference and that if we are to grow in wholeness and freedom, discernment of the movements of the Spirit is essential. One of the best known and loved illustrations of this discernment is the following: it is characteristic of the power of Christ to be like the sound of a drop of water hitting a sponge, while it is characteristic of the power of the evil spirit to be like the sound of a drop of water hitting a stone. The picture of Ignatius on the front of the book about him in the Classics of Western Spirituality is of him holding a sponge in one hand and a stone in the other, with a drop of water descending toward each.

Ignatius was clear that if prayer was given up for some reason, the only way of praying that was not to be abandoned was the "daily examen." He called it examination of conscience, but scholars over the years have agreed that he intended it to be an examination of consciousness. That word came into existence through the discipline of psychology and is much closer to the intentions of Ignatius. The practice of the daily examen, suggested by the director throughout the exercises but also encouraged upon returning home, is obviously daily, at the end of the day, to look back over the day to discern where you were aware of consolation or desolation, or when you were aware of the presence of God and when you were not. Since God is always present, you may ask, "Where was I?" This practice begins with the awareness of God's light and love so that it is not a time of harsh judgment. Then allowing the Holy Spirit to remind you of at least one happening during the day, especially if there were emotions, you may spend some time with God discerning together what was going on, going more deeply into the feelings. It is a holy practice, with essential practical awareness as the main benefit, as you then look toward the future to discern how you might be more aware of God's presence tomorrow and perhaps respond more lovingly to whatever happens.

The rest of the exercises are also of great value. The third week covers the rest of the life of Jesus through Holy Week and the crucifixion. The fourth week includes the resurrection, many appearances of Christ, the ascension, and concludes with encouragement to increase one's love for God and move into service of God and God's people. The third and fourth weeks have exercises characteristic of the unitive way.

It seems evident that the exercises of the fourth week could just as easily be said to be characteristic of the newly added "Plus One," the unitive/active way, as most often the retreatant completes the thirty-day spiritual exercises with a strong desire to serve God and God's people. After experiencing the deep love of God, spending time looking intently at Christ throughout his life, including his death and resurrection, the retreatant now longs to serve God however God leads.

It is tempting to write more about the exercises because of the incredible value of the content, but perhaps only two more points are essential before moving on. Ignatius is intentionally terse in order to make this process flexible. Differing opinions and understandings of proper use have been abundant since it was first used. Those who make the exercises are not turned into Jesuits. On the contrary, a Dominican becomes a better Dominican. A married woman with children becomes a more devoted married woman with children. A CEO of a business becomes a better CEO. In annotation 15, the director is cautioned to let the Creator deal directly with the creature, encouraging the director to stay out of the way. God is front and center, and the relationship with God is the entire purpose of the retreat. The retreatant is led to make choices based on whatever is for the greater glory of God. This graced process, used for a half century to form men and women of God, is mostly about encouraging this ongoing mutual exchange of love with God, the unitive way setting up the overflow into the unitive/active way.

Shorter formats of the exercises are offered to continue the graces received. It is said that a thirty-day retreat will last one for a lifetime. An eight-day retreat format will last a year. There are also weekend retreats with the format of using the imagination to put oneself in the gospel story.

Ignatius wanted this experience to be available to all and realized that some might not be able to be away from home for thirty days due to work or family responsibilities. His nineteenth note, commonly known as the nineteenth annotation, or the "retreat in everyday life," states that one may remain at home using a different format. The retreatant spends ninety minutes a day in prayer with the Scripture passages given by the director and meets with the director weekly for an hour over the course of thirty weeks, with breaks for Christmas and Easter. There are obvious benefits to both ways, as in the thirty-day version the retreatant must return home and then integrate the gleanings into everyday life when there are not five hours a day to pray. Both formats are widely used and prove to be most beneficial.

The exercises were published in 1548, twenty-six years after Ignatius began writing them, and are considered his most famous work today. The finished version contains the core of his spiritual genius. The rest of his writings can be considered commentaries on the exercises. Millions of copies have been printed. Since 1616, the exercises have been required for all Jesuits. Other orders also require novices to make the exercises before taking final vows. As we can see, the exercises are as relevant today as they were then, for Christians of all denominations, not just Roman Catholics.

Reflection with Ignatius

Settle In

Take a few moments to settle in. Look around. Listen. Notice what you notice. Feel the chair supporting you and your feet on the floor. Get comfortable. Stretch a bit if that helps. Take a deep breath or two to let your body help your mind slow down. Be aware of God's face turned toward you in love, right here, now. *Behold God beholding you in love.* When you are settled in, move to the options below.

1. In the introduction to this book you will find a writing attributed to Pedro Arrupe, SJ, Superior General. Reflect on it, noticing the phrases that stand out, that catch your attention, that "sparkle." Reflect on your life and where you see the truth of it.

2. Aware of the conversion story of Ignatius, reflect on your own. What other narratives were enticing you at the time? What was it like to choose a life in Christ instead of the other?

3. The interior life of Ignatius was a driving force. Ask the Holy Spirit to remind you of a time when your love connection with God helped you be firm when tempted to please others instead of God.

4. The "Principle and Foundation" encourages the pilgrim, the one making the exercises, to have indifference between long life and short, health and sickness, wealth and poverty, and good reputation and bad reputation. Does one seem more difficult to you? If it resonates, ask God for the grace to choose whatever is for the greater praise and glory of God.

5. Rest in God's presence without words, opening yourself to whatever God has for you.

6. If it is true for you, conclude your reflection time with gratitude.

7

The Classic Three Ways Plus One as Found in the Writings of John Calvin

JOHN CALVIN WAS BORN Jean Cauvin in July of 1509 in Noyon, Picardy, France. He was a French theologian, pastor, and reformer in Geneva during the Protestant Reformation. He was the principal figure of the system called Calvinism. Originally trained as a humanist lawyer, he broke with the Roman Catholic Church around 1530. After religious tension provoked a violent uprising against Protestantism in France, Calvin fled to Basil, Switzerland. There, in 1536, he published the first edition of his seminal work, *The Institutes of the Christian Religion.* He was recruited to help reform the church in Geneva, where he died in 1564.

"Love" language is curiously absent in the writings of Calvin. The word "love" does not even appear in the subject index at the back of the Classics of Western Spirituality book on Calvin. His lack of "love" language may be due in part to the fact that he was a very private person. There are few writings by Calvin or by others about Calvin revealing his inner life of piety. Scholars know Calvin best for his intellectual pursuits expressed often in what some might call "cold logic." He was a master at taking complicated ideas and creating a schema so that others could understand. This mission was central to his service as pastor in the church, to help his congregations grasp who God was and what God was doing in their lives, their relationship with God. The concept of a relationship with God is a more common one than that of loving God.

Calvin's phrase "engrafted into God" describes Calvin's own experience as a believer, as well as the life of all believers in the church. The inclusion of the body of believers may be a factor in reducing the personal love language. Calvin saw all Christians as part of the church. He was never individualistic. His writing was personal, but personal within the larger sense of community. Today's world is so individualistic that often Calvin's writings are seen to be less personal today than they were perceived in his time.

McKee says it well in the introduction to her book about Calvin's pastoral piety: "Although Calvin's theology is regarded as primarily intellectual, he himself put the greater weight on the heart; heart and head must go together but the heart is more important."[1] Calvin was clear that the creature's love for God is always a response to God's love. Once the reader can recognize what Calvin is saying, Calvin's love for his Lord is evident throughout his writings.

One beautiful example of Calvin's love for his Lord is evident in his personal crest: a flaming heart on an outstretched open hand. These words are inscribed on it: "My heart I give Thee, Lord, eagerly and entirely."[2] A heart aflame and a mind renewed describes him well. For Calvin, faith and prayer are central to the relationship with God, and both must first be inward. However, they may not remain hidden. They must transform the community and the world as they transform each praying believer. The word "piety" describes Calvin's spirituality, and in his piety his love for God is second only to God's love for him. Calvin's love for God includes a personal love for God that is central, always within a larger corporate love for God in the church.

Calvin saw his purpose as that of challenging others to realize that "their true happiness consists in devotion to God for God's glory; that their salvation is assured by Christ's grace; and so their lives will be transformed by the power of the Holy Spirit."[3] Calvin's belief that true happiness comes from loving God resounds with Bernard's view earlier in chapter four.

1. Calvin, *Pastoral Piety*, 3.
2. Kerr, *By John Calvin*, 19.
3. Calvin, *Pastoral Piety*, xi.

What appears to be the culmination of the process for our medieval brothers and sisters, union with God, is the starting place for Calvin. Now, Calvin loved the lives and writings of Bernard and Augustine and agreed with them that God's love initiates the relationship between God and humankind. God's love is always first because God is love. It is who God is. God's love cannot be earned; it is freely given. Calvin allows for no works righteousness, seeing that this exhausting futile endeavor was already too fully developed in the Roman Catholic Church.

The movement in the journey of faith is still evident as one grows, becoming more the creature God desires to create. Would Calvin have found an argument in Augustine, Bernard, Catherine, Ignatius, or Teresa? Would they have agreed with Calvin that all movement toward God is initiated by God? The answer is yes, but they would not have placed the creature in a place of union with God at the beginning. For the medieval mind, there loomed the concept of working for one's salvation, with much to be done by the creature, by God's grace of course, on the way to union, beginning with the purgative way.

For Calvin, the purgative way is prevalent, though not in order to achieve salvation. Salvation is a gift, by God's grace, for Calvin, but there are certain responses the creature makes to that gift. One that is central in the writings of Calvin is self-denial. He says that the sum of the Christian life is self-denial, remembering that I am not my own, but am to conform my life to the way God wants. In order to be free to seek first the glory of God, Christians must first renounce self-love. This may remind us of the woman on retreat who said the Christian journey is all about letting go. Above all Calvin wanted to nurture piety in his followers, and he encouraged them in the purgative way, the purging of the old in order to make way for the new.

A hymn attributed to John Calvin, "I Greet Thee, Who My Sure Redeemer Art" (see "Hymns" at the end of this chapter) provides strong evidence of his living and teaching the Classic Three Ways. Looking at the first stanza, one sees the purgative way in the need of the believer. The one singing is aware of being poor, worthless, and needing the Savior to take all idle grief and foolish cares. In stanza six, we not only see again the adjective "poor" but also "wretched" to describe the singer, asking for pity and pardon and salvation.

A connection to the Roman Catholic Church is found in stanzas six and seven. The words are very similar to "Salve Regina," the song to Mary that Trappist monks sing every evening during Compline today (see "Hymns"), though Calvin's lyrics are sung to Jesus. The last three stanzas are not in the current Presbyterian hymnal version of this same hymn, but if the older eight-stanza version of the hymn is authentic, then Calvin was aware of these words. One cannot assume that he knew this song to Mary, but it is probable that he had seen or heard these words.

The preface to "Commentary on Psalms" provides one of the rare views into Calvin's personal life within his writing. The Psalms were his prayer book, so his heart for God shines forth throughout the commentary, but there is strong evidence of the purgative way in his preface. He is writing to encourage his followers to read the Psalms, to use them for prayer, and says,

> But here the prophets themselves, seeing they are exhibited to us as speaking to God, and laying open all their inmost thoughts and affections, call, or rather draw, each of us to the examination of himself in particular, in order that none of the many infirmities to which we are subject, and of the many vices with which we abound may remain concealed. It is certainly a rare and single advantage, when all lurking places are discovered, and the heart is brought into the light, purged from that most baneful infection, hypocrisy.[4]

Calvin in this preface encourages self-examination, a cornerstone of Ignatian spirituality (the daily examen) in order to let go, to confess, to purge the vices that are concealed. He even moves toward the next step, the illuminative way, when he says the heart is brought into the light.

A personal letter from Calvin to William Farel, a close friend, shows his profound submission to God's leading through

---

4. Calvin, *Pastoral Piety*, 56.

other people. Calvin uses a phrase common in his own expression of faith, and interestingly also very common in the spiritual exercises of St. Ignatius of Loyola: "What is most for the glory of God."[5] This phrase is the epitome of the purgative way, the Gethsemane prayer, not my way, but yours. Here is another example from the same letter.

> But when I remember I am not my own, I offer up my heart, presented as a sacrifice to the Lord. Therefore, I submit my will and my affections, subdued and held fast, to the obedience of God; and whenever I am at a loss for counsel of my own, I submit myself to those by whom I hope that the Lord will speak to me.[6]

Calvin is no stranger to letting go, to opening himself to God and to those God sends to counsel him. This letting go, this purgative way, empties out some space, making room for the illuminative way to bring forth new ideas.

These paragraphs of the *Institutes* are essential not only to the understanding of the Classic Three Ways, but also to identify the beginning place for Calvin, which is God's holiness. Paragraph two is titled, "Without knowledge of God there is no knowledge of self."[7]

> We are not thus convinced (of our unrighteousness, foulness, folly, impurity) if we look merely to ourselves and not also to the Lord, who is the sole standard by which this judgment must be measured.[8]

Just looking inward is not enough. There must be a measuring rod, which alone is God. Calvin brings home the fact of the necessity of God's holiness, God's otherness. After a while it becomes clear that all who move along this process of the Classic Three Ways must begin with the image of God, the holiness and goodness of this One against whom all else is measured. Though it may not have been mentioned explicitly in the earlier chapters,

5. Calvin, *Pastoral Piety*, 51.
6. Calvin, *Pastoral Piety*, 51
7. Calvin, *Institutes*, 1.1.2, 37.
8. Calvin, *Institutes*, 1.1.2, 37.

Augustine, Bernard, Catherine, and Ignatius all had experiences of God that brought them to their knees. It is the starting point before the purgative way, the awakening.

The third paragraph of chapter 1 is called "Man before God's majesty" and in it, Calvin says, "Scripture commonly represents the saints as stricken and overcome whenever they felt the presence of God."[9]

Chapters 6 through 10 of book three are worth noting. They pursue the concept that love of righteousness is not our nature. However, when one compares oneself to God, one is moved to let go of one's own way, and Calvin repeats his earlier words, "We are not our own."[10] He continues encouraging self-denial, self-renunciation, and self-forgetfulness as the way to call us back to humility, abundantly quoting Paul's letters and other Scripture. With this hope, we can move to the illuminative way.

Examples of this second way, the illuminative way, are not as prevalent in Calvin's writings, as often the believer is aware of the sin, confesses, and then moves into closeness with God. There are a few examples however, such as in the preface to "The Day of Prayer" which invites believers to be alert, to look for God's mercies every day. The main theme is repentance (purgative way) as Calvin calls Christians to read the signs of their instruction. Calvin's high regard for and use of Scripture is another way he reveals indications of the illuminative way, seeing with the heart. As believers are drawn to read Scripture, God's Spirit enlightens them in their hearts in their reading, and they experience God in a profound way. In this context, note Calvin's hymn again, this time looking at stanza two for the illuminative way in the words "shine your light." It is the natural progression.

Calvin's prayer of defense, written so beautifully in his letter to Sadoleto, expresses his frustration that Scripture is not available to all people, as he says, "Your word, which ought to have

9. Calvin, *Institutes*, 1.1.3, 38.
10. Calvin, *Institutes*, 3.7.1, 690.

shone on all your people like a lamp, was for us taken away or at least suppressed."[11]

These words come to mind, "To this extent we are prompted by our own ills to contemplate the good things of God, and we cannot seriously aspire to him, before we begin to become displeased with ourselves."[12] The movement from an awareness of God's holiness, through displeasure with ourselves, and finally to looking to God for help represents the natural progression of the faith journey. The word "light" is often an indication of the illuminative way as seen in these words that Calvin quotes from Paul's letter to the Corinthians: "God, who 'ordered light to shine out of darkness, now has shone in our hearts to give the light of the knowledge of the glory of God in the face of Jesus Christ' (II Cor. 4:6)."[13]

Note that he says, "shone in our *hearts*," not *heads*. In the next section, entitled "The gospel preaches the revealed Christ," Calvin writes more about revelation for believers, indicating the illuminative way. It is in this section that Calvin offers this line, revealing his sense of the obvious. "There is no need to heap up passages to prove something so fully known, 'By his advent Christ has brought life and immortality to light through the gospel' (II Tim. 1:10)."[14]

In book one of the *Institutes*, Calvin writes about the knowledge of God, the Creator, and provides an illustration of the illuminative way, again emphasizing that it is not just head knowledge but also a deeper visceral awareness.

> No drop will be found either of wisdom and light, or of righteousness or power or rectitude or of genuine truth, which does not flow from God, and of which God is not the cause. Thus, we may learn to await and seek all these things from God, and thankfully to ascribe them, once received, to God.[15]

---

11. Calvin, *Pastoral Piety*, 47.

12. Calvin, *Institutes*, 1.1.1, 36.

13. Calvin, *Institutes*, 2.9.1, 424.

14. Calvin, *Institutes*, 2.9.2, 425.

15. Calvin, *Institutes*, 1.2.1, 41.

Ford Lewis Battles, in the preface to *The Piety of John Calvin*, suggests that the three "moments" of prayer are directly from Calvin in the *Institutes* and that they are another way of saying the Classic Three Ways. Battles's three moments of prayer are simply: our realization of our own inability, or need; our discovery of Christ's power; and our appropriation of Christ's power through grace. While Battles does not identify these moments of prayer with the first three steps of the Twelve Steps of Alcoholics Anonymous, they coincide precisely. When we come upon truth, we discover it in many forms everywhere. In Calvin's words we read,

> From those matters so far discussed, we clearly see how destitute and devoid of all good things man is, and how he lacks all aids to salvation. It was afterward explained to us that the Lord willingly and freely reveals himself in his Christ. For in Christ he offers all happiness in place of our misery, all wealth in place of our neediness; in him he opens to us the heavenly treasures that our whole faith may contemplate his beloved Son, our whole expectation depend upon him and our whole hope cleave to and rest in him.[16]

The purgative way is evident, as we lack all good things and must give up on our own way of getting them and look to God. The illuminative way is the revealing that God does in Christ. The contemplating and resting are the unitive way. There are few examples of the illuminative way by itself, but this one is an exception. "They whose eyes God has opened surely learn it by heart, that in God's light they may see light."[17]

There are some instances where Calvin describes the process of the faith journey using the Classic Three Ways terminology, occasionally adding the fourth, in one sentence, and thus showing the continuity of this thread woven through from the Middle Ages to the Reformation.

> When I say they embraced the Word to be united more closely to God, I do not mean that general mode of

16. Calvin, *Institutes*, 3.20.1, 850.
17. Calvin, *Institutes*, 3.20.1, 850.

communication which is diffused through heaven and earth and all the creatures of the world. For although it quickens all things, each according to the measure of its nature, it still does not free them from the exigency of corruption. Rather, I mean that special mode which both illumines the souls of the pious into the knowledge of God, and in a sense, joins them to God. Adam, Abel, Noah, Abraham, and the other patriarchs cleaved to God by such illumination of the Word.[18]

These words of Calvin are good preparation for the unitive way. What's unique to Calvin is that the baseline, the starting point for Christians is union with Christ. This union, so prevalent in the writings of Calvin, brings him to greater clarity about the distinction between the Creator and the creature. They are not the same even when they are in union. The Creator is always Lord over the creation.

A distinction needs to be made between "union with Christ" and the "unitive way." The unitive way is an existential experience of the believer with God in Christ. For Calvin, "union with Christ" means that we are engrafted into Christ. This perspective, of already being one with Christ, does not mean that we "have arrived" and are fully formed as followers of Christ. However, we have seen that the unitive way is also found in Calvin, in the form of experience. From Tamburello again,

> I find Calvin's "burning interest" to be precisely "Christian Experience." Calvin makes it clear that he wants nothing to do with any purely intellectual knowledge of God; that, indeed, the promotion of piety is what concerns him most deeply.[19]

Returning to Calvin's hymn, stanza four speaks of the unitive way in the words "Thy sweet unity," revealing an affective expression of union with Christ. The progress through the hymn is much like the progress through the Classic Three Ways.

18. Calvin, *Institutes*, 2.10.7, 434.
19. Tamburello, *Union with Christ*, 104.

Calvin begins book three of the *Institutes* describing how the believer can receive the grace of Christ. He provides a delightful picture of the Trinity, explaining our union with Christ as being only within the Trinity. The Holy Spirit unites humankind to Christ so that Christ can share what he has received from the Father.

> We are said to be engrafted into Christ and are to put on Christ; for as I have said, all that he possesses is nothing to us until we grow into one body with him. It is true that we obtain this by faith. Yet since we see that not all indiscriminately embrace that communion with Christ, which is offered through the gospel, reason itself teaches us to climb higher and to examine into the secret energy of the Spirit, by which we come to enjoy Christ and all his benefits.[20]

Here it is evident that there is more to the journey in Christ, as the believer needs to grow into one body with him. We can be in union, engrafted, but there is more, and there is always more, moving toward the unitive way. Continuing, Calvin gives more detail about the relationship of Christ with the Holy Spirit and what difference that makes to Christians.

God the Father gives us the Holy Spirit for Christ's sake, so that God can make disciples of those who were previously destitute and empty of heavenly doctrine. Calvin speaks of the gifts of the Spirit and the character, or fruit of the Spirit, and that Christ would have come in vain had he not had this power. Then he confirms this union by saying, "This unique life which the Son of God inspires in his own so that they become one with him, Paul here contrasts with that natural life which is common also to the wicked."[21] Calvin presents the unitive way as the natural next step once the Spirit has illumined the believer. "Christ, when he illumines us into faith by the power of his Spirit, at the same time so engrafts us into his body that we become partakers of every good."[22] For Calvin, being in union, being joined to Christ, is *the* act of faith taken by Christ,

20. Calvin, *Institutes*, 3.1.1, 537.

21. Calvin, *Institutes*, 3.1.2, 539.

22. Calvin, *Institutes*, 3.2.35, 583.

all gift for the believer. "It does not reconcile us to God at all unless it joins us to Christ."[23]

For Calvin, this process is an "already, not yet" concept. The statement "We have been saved, we are being saved, and we will be saved" is another expression of this concept. The idea of union with Christ in the theology of Calvin begins with God engrafting a person into Christ, without any required response or agreement from the person; however, while abiding in Christ, that same person may be making choices that are not in conformity with Christ. Calvin explains it this way:

> Christ is not outside us but dwells within us. Not only does he cleave to us by an indivisible bond of fellowship, but with a wonderful communion, day by day, he grows more and more into one body with us, until he becomes completely one with us. Yet I do not deny what I stated above: that certain interruptions of faith occasionally occur, according as its weakness is violently buffeted hither and thither; so, in the thick darkness of temptations its light is snuffed out. Yet whatever happens, it ceases not its earnest quest for God.[24]

Another difference between Calvin and his medieval fore-runners is the emphasis Calvin puts on being engrafted into Christ in baptism. The medieval thinkers were quick to say that baptism began a relationship between the person and Christ, but they did not call that union. All would say that every step of faith from baptism on is by God's grace, so here is evidence of continuity between Calvin's understanding and that of earlier believers.

In order to compare union with Christ for Calvin with the union with Christ for Bernard and others prior to the Protestant Reformation, we can see that the experience of being engrafted into Christ, by faith, is true, and is part of the definition of what it means to be a believer, but this engrafting is not a unitive experience in which the deepest longings of the soul are satisfied.

---

23. Calvin, *Institutes*, 3.2.30, 576.
24. Calvin, *Institutes*, 3.2.24, 570.

Dennis Tamburello's book *Union with Christ: John Calvin and the Mysticism of St. Bernard* considers whether Calvin's "union with Christ" is truly mysticism, and in the conclusion he says that it basically is, if others would not go to such lengths to define so narrowly words such as "mysticism."[25] Adding to the "already, not yet" concept, Tamburello suggests that for Calvin, the union of justification is in a sense total, while the union of sanctification is always partial and growing. "The notion of progress in sanctification is a frequent one in Calvin."[26]

Calvin's devotion to God, his love for Christ, is the essence of his piety, and he uses Paul's language of growing into Christ: more of Christ, less of me. In a seminar class on medieval and Reformed spirituality, the professor, Dr. Philip Krey, spoke of Calvin's picking up some of the devotion of the twelfth century, since there were many spiritual options from which the Reformers chose. After the Reformation, choices became more limited. So, we ask, for Calvin is the unitive way more than the engrafting that occurs at baptism? The answer is yes! However, it comes with the underlying belief that is foundational for Calvin and shows a distinct difference from the medieval understanding—that this closest mystical union with Christ is already fully available to the believer at baptism—and for Calvin it is more a matter of growing into it than starting from scratch.

> That joining together of Head and members, that indwelling of Christ in our hearts, in short, that mystical union, are accorded by us the highest degree of importance, so that Christ, having been made ours, makes us sharers with him in the gifts with which he has been endowed. We do not, therefore, contemplate him outside ourselves from afar in order that his righteousness may be imputed to us but because we put on Christ and are engrafted into his body, in short, because he deigns to make us one with him. For this reason, we glory that we have fellowship of righteousness with him.[27]

25. Tamburello, *Union with Christ*, 110.

26. Tamburello, *Union with Christ*, 101.

27. Calvin, *Institutes*, 3.11.10, 737.

Before moving to the fourth way, the unitive/active way, let us return to our beginning comments about the first and greatest commandment, to love God with all of who we are. This unitive way is the highest form of life in Christ, perhaps what Paul meant by being caught up into the third heaven (2 Cor 12:2). For our medieval brothers and sisters as well as for our brother Calvin, there are times when the Christian is aware of such great gratitude welling up inside as the fruit of this process of the Classic Three Ways, by God's grace. The Scripture passage that comes to mind is that which recounts the dinner with Simon the pharisee and the woman with the alabaster jar. Jesus asks Simon, "Who will love more, the one who is forgiven fifty or the one forgiven five hundred?" (Luke 7:41). This profound gratitude for sins forgiven is a natural result of moving through these Classic Three Ways, knowing that it is all grace. This experience is full of joy that cannot be contained. Like the woman with the alabaster jar, her love full of gratefulness pours out on Christ.

When we are in this place of union with God, God, in delight, tosses us back into the world to love as God loves, and we meet this gesture with the same delight. It is not even a conscious choice. It is a natural overflow from living in God's love to loving our neighbor and serving that neighbor as God leads.

A revered Protestant theology professor was relatively sure there would not be any Classic Three Ways in Calvin's *Institutes*, his most acclaimed work. However, with some sleuthing, it was unveiled. Examples of this unitive/active way as well as the other three ways are abundant in Calvin. He does not specifically mention the need for the Classic Three Ways in order to love our brothers and sisters, but it is evident in his writing that self-renunciation is our only hope, and the process is descriptive of many in the faith journey.

Ford Lewis Battles, again, in a note that he writes in *Piety*, says that Calvin spoke of *pietas* as the root of *caritas* in his sermon on Ezekiel and that he developed the concept of a relationship between our reverential attitude toward God and our attitude toward neighbor in a sermon on Deuteronomy. The best hope we have of loving our neighbor comes from the central theme of Calvin mentioned above, that we share the gifts of Christ because we are in Christ. We can love our neighbor with the love of Christ in us. Calvin emphasizes the connection between the two commands in "Love of neighbor is not dependent upon the manner of humankind but looks to God,"[28] a paragraph in the *Institutes*. Here he encourages believers to see God in the neighbor. The image of God in the neighbor is worthy of your giving yourself and all your possessions. We are called "to look upon the image of God in them, which cancels and effaces their transgressions, and with its beauty and dignity allures us to love and embrace them."[29] Seeing our neighbor in God provides an even larger perspective, revealing that all belong; we are all in God.

Therefore, as we are rooted and grounded in God, we will love our neighbors and ourselves for God's sake, not out of some need to impress others or gain anything for ourselves. Our love for God is especially not in order to find favor with God. The love with which we are to love is God's love within us and it is sheer gift because of who God is.

> You see that our righteousness is not in us but in Christ, that we possess it only because we are partakers in Christ; indeed, with him we possess all its riches. And this does not contradict what he teaches elsewhere, that sin has been condemned for sin in Christ's flesh that the righteousness of the law might be fulfilled in us. The only fulfillment he alludes to is that which we obtain through imputation. For in such a way does the Lord Christ share his righteousness with us that, in some wonderful manner, he pours into us enough of his power to meet the judgment of God.[30]

Though Calvin challenged the old ways and called believers to new ways of understanding much of Scripture and tradition, there was not a clean break between medieval spirituality and Reformed

28. Calvin, *Institutes*, 3.7.6, 696.
29. Calvin, *Institutes*, 3.7.6, 697.
30. Calvin, *Institutes*, 3.11.23, 753.

theology. The Classic Three Ways (Plus One) are woven throughout the *Institutes* and other writings, especially when speaking of the relationship of the Creator with the creature. This mutual exchange of love as essential for life is evident in Calvin's writings.

Hymns

"I Greet Thee, Who My Sure Redeemer Art"
Attributed to John Calvin in 1545[31]

I greet Thee, who my sure Redeemer art,
My only Trust, and Saviour of my heart!
Who so much toil and woe
And Pain didst undergo,
For my poor worthless sake;
And pray Thee, from our hearts,
All idle grief and smarts
And foolish cares to take.

Thou art the King of mercy and of grace.
Reigning omnipotent in every place:
So come, O King! And deign
Within our hearts to reign,
And our whole being sway;
Shine in us by Thy light,
And lead us to the height
Of Thy pure, heavenly day.

Thou art the Life by which alone we live,
And all our substance and our strength receive:
Comfort us by Thy Faith
Against the pains of death;
Sustain us by Thy power;
Let not our fears prevail,
Nor our hearts faint or fail,
When comes the trying hour.

31. *The Presbyterian Hymnal*, #457.

Thou art the true and perfect gentleness,
No harshness hast Thou, and no bitterness:
>>Make us to taste and prove,
>>Make us adore and love
>The sweet grace found in Thee;
>>With longing to abide
>>Ever at Thy dear side,
In Thy sweet unity.

Our hope is in no other save in Thee,
Our faith is built upon Thy promise free;
>>Come, and our hope increase,
>>Comfort and give us peace,
>Make us so strong and sure,
>>That we shall conquerors, be,
>>And well and patiently
Shall every ill endure.

Poor, banished exiles, wretched sons of Eve,
Full of all sorrows, unto Thee we grieve!
>>To Thee we bring our sighs,
>>Our groanings and our cries:
>Thy pity, Lord, we crave;
>>We take the sinner's place,
>>And pray Thee, of Thy grace,
To pardon and to save.

Turn Thy sweet eyes upon our low estate,
Our Mediator and our Advocate,
>>Propitiator best!
>>Give us that vision blest,
>The God of gods most high!
>>And let us, by Thy right,
>>Enter the blessed light
And glories of the sky!

Oh, pitiful and gracious as Thou art,
The lovely Bridegroom of the holy heart,
　　Lord Jesus Christ, meet Thou
　　The Antichrist, our foe,
　In all his cruel truth!
　　Thy Spirit give, that we
　　May, in true verity,
Follow Thy words of truth.

"Salve Regina"
　Copied from Benedictine Compline Service
　at Mepkin Abbey, Moncks Corner, SC

Hail, Holy Queen, Mother all merciful!

Our life, our sweetness, and our hope we hail you!

To you do we cry, poor banished children of Eve.

To you we send our sighs of mourning and weeping
　in this lonely valley of tears.

Turn, then, your eyes, most gracious advocate.

O turn your eyes, so full of love and tenderness upon us sinners;

And Jesus, the most blessed fruit of your virgin womb,

Show us when this lowly exile is ended.

O clement, O loving, O most sweet Virgin Mary.

Reflection with Calvin

Settle In

Take a few moments to settle in. Look around. Listen. Notice what you notice. Feel the chair supporting you and your feet on the floor. Get comfortable. Stretch a bit if that helps. Take a deep breath or two to let your body help your mind slow down. Be aware of God's face turned toward you in love, right here, now. *Behold God beholding you in love.* When you are settled in, move to the options below.

1. In the lives of both Augustine and Calvin the heart was a strong symbol. Do you notice any similarities in their lives of faith?

2. Aware of Calvin's crest with the inscription "I give you my heart," what might you create for a crest for your life?

3. Enjoy the hymn of Calvin. Read it slowly, savoring the words. Notice which words or phrases catch your attention. Soak in those words. Water them for your own journey.

4. As for the differences in understanding union with God, a formidable topic for conversation in the sixteenth century, it seems that the crux of it is the difference between justification and sanctification. Looking at your own life, ponder the desire of Calvin to grow into Christ, to use Paul's words, "to have more of Christ and less of me."

5. Rest in God without words, opening yourself to whatever God has for you.

6. If it is true for you, conclude your reflection time with gratitude.

8

The Classic Three Ways Plus One
as Found in *The Interior Castle*
by Teresa of Avila

WHILE THERE ARE MANY more heroes of faith whose lives and
writings could be included here, those already named, Augustine,
Bernard, Catherine, Ignatius, and John Calvin, provide us a wide
range of Christians whose lives and works have formed the lives of
believers down through many centuries. With the emphasis in this
book on the mutual exchange of love between God and humankind, especially as illustrated in the fourth way, the unitive/active
way in the Classic Three Ways Plus One, one more faith reformer
must be included.

Teresa of Avila was born Teresa Sanchez de Cepeda y Ahumada in March of 1515 in Avila, Castile (Spain today). Her grand-
father was a Jewish man converted to Christianity, which caused
her and her family to be of suspicion during the Inquisition. Her
father, Alonso Sanchez, was a successful wool merchant. Teresa's
mother, Beatriz de Ahumada y Cuevas, intentionally raised Teresa as a pious Christian. Teresa was fascinated by the lives of the
saints. Their lives inspired her to run away from home when she
was seven. She convinced her brother Rodrigo to run off with her
to find martyrdom among the Moors. Their uncle stopped them as
he was returning to town.

Being born during the reign of the Catholic monarchs Fer-
dinand and Isabella, Teresa saw Spain at a time when it was very

involved in the conquest of new lands. Her brother Rodrigo went to America on a ship in 1535, never to return home, as he was killed in battle. Teresa's mother died when Teresa was only eleven. Teresa was grief-stricken, as they were very close. She turned to Mary of Nazareth, the mother of Jesus, to be her spiritual mother and had a great devotion to Mary all her life.

As mentioned in the chapter on Ignatius of Loyola, Teresa of Avila made significant contributions to the Roman Catholic reform. Teresa's life was full of activity reforming the Carmelite order which originated in Palestine in the twelfth century. By the thirteenth century, members of the order had migrated all over Europe. Over the years the strict rules of these convents had become lax and were known for their social life, as the nuns entertained visitors in their parlors. Many wealthy visitors gave lavish gifts which were accepted gratefully.

Teresa was most likely taught to read and write at home. In 1531, she was sent as a boarder to an Augustinian convent for education, but the focus was on becoming a wife and mother, with such studies as cooking and sewing. She left there after eighteen months. In 1535, Teresa entered the Carmelite Convent of the Incarnation in Avila and took the name Teresa of Jesus. She became an invalid and during these years developed a great love for mental prayer, prayer without speaking. In those days the common opinion was that the brains of women were not capable of mental prayer, and her spiritual director commanded her to stop. She did return to mental prayer after about three years, but she was confused and flailed about in her faith journey for about forty years, trying to find her way between her relationship to the world and her relationship with God.

There was a deep division within Teresa that continued until she had a dramatic conversion experience, seeing Christ in a vision. This experience of Christ led her to become aware of the need of reform within the Carmelite order, thinking it was spiritually harmful that the convent was not fully enclosed and was so open to the world. With the encouragement of the writings of St. Peter Alcantara, she started a new order, OCD, Order of Carmelites,

Discalced, or barefoot, for nuns who would observe the strict original Carmelite rule. There was significant opposition, but eventually she founded the Convent of St. Joseph in Avila, which was followed by many other reformed houses. She was elected abbess but always took the seat next to the chair for the abbess, saying that Mary, the Mother of Jesus, was the true abbess. Another well-known reformer, much younger than she, John of the Cross, worked with her to found reformed houses for men. She had been praying for two friars to help with the men's houses, and because of John's short stature, she said God sent her one and a half men when John and another friar arrived. In 1567 they opened two reformed houses for men.

A favorite adjective for Teresa of Avila is "spunky." You get a sense of her personality when you think of what it means to be a spunky woman now, much less in sixteenth-century Spain. Teresa may be best known for her ability to combine a life of great creative activity with a profound depth of mystical experience in prayer. She was most uncomfortable with the public "favors" she received from God in prayer and would ask her sisters to please pull her down to the floor when she began to levitate. She said that the reason God gave her these special favors was because of her weak faith, in order to reveal his love for her. A delightful story tells of Teresa in the garden when she received a visit from the child Jesus. He asked her to tell him her name. To which she replied, "I am Teresa of Jesus." She asked him, "And who are you?" He replied, "I am Jesus of Teresa."

Her writings and her role as abbess of the monastery revealed her love for God, but it was so much more than that. It was who she was, her very essence. "It was with her whole being that she gave herself to a life of union with God."[1]

Now let us turn to *The Interior Castle*. It was written in 1577 and is her most mature work. Because it was written in her later years, it seems to answer some of the questions left unanswered in her earlier books. Though Teresa's writing is not as linear as the writing of Ignatius, we are allowed entry into her inmost thoughts.

1. Payne, *Paul-Marie of the Cross*, 35.

She takes the reader on many circuitous paths on her way through the mansions, where God dwells at the center of the soul.

Teresa was resistant to writing this, her best-known book, because she felt she had nothing more to say about prayer that was not already in her other books. She also said that God had not given her the power or the desire to write, but she would write anyway because she knew "the power obedience has of making things easy that seem impossible."[2] She was able to complete the book in only four weeks, not counting the five-month break in the middle due to illness and other problems such as resistance to the reform by those within the order.

The image for the spiritual journey, the path of growth in faith, that Teresa uses here is that of a castle inside the soul of every person. The book is not a full treatise on mystical prayer as much as it is a road she has traveled, and she is clear that others may travel a different path. It is thought that she most likely did not actually endure some of the earlier mansions, for "by God's grace she was preserved from childhood from any grievous sin and gross imperfection."[3] But her writings ring with truth, as she consulted many others as she was writing to confirm the authenticity of what she was writing.

There are seven mansions within the soul, each one going deeper within, with the seventh one being where God dwells, full of warmth and light. In her words we read:

> I thought of a soul resembling a castle, formed of a single diamond or a very transparent crystal, and containing many rooms, just as in heaven there are many mansions. If we reflect, sisters, we shall see that the soul of the just man is but a paradise, in which God tells us he takes his delight.[4]

The beauty of the image provided in the first few pages of the first mansion is striking. Here Teresa reminds the reader that

2. Teresa, *Interior Castle*, 35.

3. Teresa, *Interior Castle*, 28.

4. Teresa, *Interior Castle*, 38.

we, that our souls, are made for God. The soul is a capacity for God. God is the center of the soul and all its beauty is because of God.[5] For Teresa, spiritual growth is a journey inward, a penetration of this castle. We can choose whether to enter or not, but the invitation still exists. God calls us, "Come to me," and welcomes us into an intimacy with God, into God's very heart.[6] God calls us and then gives us the very capacity to come. We have a choice. On God's side it is total gift, but there is an initial lack of intimacy between the soul and God because of all the noise of the outer courtyard!

Now, moving into the mansions, we will begin with the courtyard of the first mansion. It is cold, dark, and clammy, full of reptiles and junk. Teresa is clear that even there we have "the power to hold converse with none other than God himself."[7] To even arrive at the outer courts of the castle, one must be a person of prayer, because that is the door of entry into the castle. On the path toward God, toward holiness, Teresa encourages the reader that the journey is about ordinary things such as kindness, courtesy, honesty, and courage.

In the second mansion she reminds us that while God is always giving God's self, we must grow to receive God. Moving through this mansion depends on generosity and courage, words that will sound familiar, as they were suggested by Ignatius for the Spiritual Exercises. Here we are called to love God with our whole heart and soul and mind. Love is not a warm feeling; it is a choosing. I have to choose to love God when I feel no attraction.[8] There is a little more light in the second dwelling, so there is more awareness of who God is, and who we are, and that we cannot do this on our own. It is hard going, as we are encouraged to bring the will into conformity with the will of God and to let go of false values and childish enjoyments.

5. Burrows, *Interior Castle Explored*, 6.

6. Burrows, *Interior Castle Explored*, 10.

7. Burrows, *Interior Castle Explored*, 11.

8. Burrows, *Interior Castle Explored*, 23.

The next mansion is full of many who are still concerned with their own spiritual image rather than becoming all God's. There is a perceived need by the pilgrim to be normal, like the others in church perhaps, with honor and graces and considerable self-esteem, rather than the humility of being nothing so that God can be all. Moving on to the fourth mansion only happens when there is a willingness to leave self behind, by God's grace. Humankind is full of self-centeredness, evident both in the sixteenth century and today, so we are given the choice, and many make the choice to remain here in the third mansion.

> God never leaves us alone and is always trying to liber-
> ate us, but the tragedy is that as the years go by, as time
> and time again we refuse this liberation, we grow more
> and more fixed in our ways. The Lord is helpless. Perhaps
> the last illness, perhaps death provides the shattering ex-
> perience which will bring the healing revelation. But it
> is a tragedy all the same, for the love of God is beating
> round us, Spirit and Fire, storming our ramparts to ef-
> fect an entrance; the kingdom is seeking a weak point
> for invasion, but no, the impregnable fortress remains
> unconquered.[9]

This third mansion is the place where there is a strong temp-tation for committed believers to stop because to go on is just too difficult, or at least too foreign, too quiet, when we are used to the noise, used to being in control, used to knowing, and we are not even halfway to the center.

The fourth mansion is the first place of unknowing, of going beyond what one can see, count, or otherwise measure. It is the beginning of mystical encounter with God's inflowing love. The Gethsemane passage comes to mind, as Jesus prayed that the cup would pass from him but then added that whatever God wanted, he would do. The self-surrender required in this mansion is not easy. It is even impossible, and a divine gift is needed. It is pure gift, something we cannot achieve for ourselves. "It is something

9. Burrows, *Interior Castle Explored*, 34.

entirely new. It is not a deepening of what has gone before, not an increasing expertise, not a continuation, but a break."[10]

This incredible gift is offered to all without exception. There are few who surrender wholly to it, some hardly at all. It is often called infused contemplation because it is a gift given by God. If we grasp what Teresa is saying, we can see it is our very lifeline, our very meaning as human beings. There is a hidden quality to this mutual indwelling, and it is humility that obtains this grace. It is in silence and letting go, and often it is not at all perceived by the one receiving the grace.

The grace given in the fourth mansion is that here we have a face to look at, the face of Jesus, and we can only really know him from within this deep encounter. Jesus becomes the cleft in the rock so we can encounter God. "The unbearable presence of God is made bearable in Jesus."[11] This fourth mansion is most likely the furthest place most believers go on this journey inward. Many do enter this mansion but choose not to dwell here because it is no longer about me and my improvements and has become all about God. It is easier to focus on what is in it for me, what can I get out of it, instead of truly handing ourselves over to God. If self-interest is not served, it just does not make sense.

Looking at the "pillars of the church" in modern times, from the outside it is not easy to know for sure if they have stopped at the third mansion because they find the unknowing of the fourth mansion frightening, or if they are living from a unitive place with God, even a unitive/active place. The proof is in hindsight as those who are working, serving only from their own resources, find themselves not to be enough. They become burned out and complain, blaming the church for overworking them. Those who are serving from the unitive place with God, who serve as God leads and with God's resources, are replenished from their deep rootedness in God. It is not ours to judge others of course, but we are invited to take note of our own lives and set our hearts on going deeper.

---

10. Burrows, *Interior Castle Explored*, 42.
11. Burrows, *Interior Castle Explored*, 60.

Ruth Burrows in her commentary of *The Interior Castle* groups the mansions such that the first three mansions are from the Old Testament of the soul, while the next three are the soul's encounter with the suffering Son of Man, sharing in his death, willing to die to self. The seventh mansion is the risen life, the life in the Spirit.

Moving into the fifth mansion is more intense than the fourth, as the pilgrim is called to stand in the blinding truth of God. God is not giving himself more fully here, but the soul has developed, by God's grace, a greater capacity to receive. There is a greater mix of divine and human work, a dance if you will. The grace of the fifth mansion is this: "It does not mean that one never fails but it does mean that the compass is always set, the will stretched toward God without any slackening."[12] Even that compass-setting is a direct effect of God; it is all gift. It is a union with Christ in his death. Here Teresa speaks of betrothal, which in her time always led to marriage, in preparation for the next mansions.

The sixth mansion is by far the longest with eleven chapters, while the next longest has four chapters. There is much repetition, and the value of the detail is not clear for the purpose of this book, so a comparison of the last three mansions may be helpful.

> The fifth ushers us into the contemplative life, the life of passionate love; the sixth is the living out of that love, the living of the surrendered heart; the seventh is the perfection of love.[13]

Surrender is central, drawing the soul away from self-interest. It is total acceptance of total dependency. Many have said that there is truly nothing that can be said about the seventh mansion. Teresa's words are flat as she tries to communicate this encounter where human words are meaningless. But one comment must be highlighted. In this final chapter Teresa explains that the purpose of all this is that one "might live like Christ and that the fruit of the marriage must be good works."[14]

12. Burrows, *Interior Castle Explored*, 83.
13. Burrows, *Interior Castle Explored*, 90.
14. Teresa, *Collected Works*, 2:278.

Stepping back now from the text to look for the Classic Three Ways Plus One, scholars are mostly agreed that the first two mansions are the purgative way, the third and fourth are the illuminative, and the rest are all unitive. The Plus One again fits easily into the process as Teresa call us to serve others as we live as branches on the vine in this mutual exchange of love. There is strong evidence that the seventh mansion is indeed not just unitive but is unitive/active. Here are the words of Teresa herself:

> This is what I want us to strive for, my Sisters; and let us desire and be occupied in prayer not for the sake of our enjoyment but so as to have this strength to serve.[15]

She is clear that once we have discovered this place of union with our holy and loving God, we will love as God loves, and that will throw us back into the world as we are now fully equipped to love God's people with God's love alive in us. This love is both qualitatively and quantitatively greater than whatever love we can muster on our own and it endures because the One in whom the love originates is infinite.

This image brings us back to the vine and the branch of John 15. As the branch is attached to the vine, the branch will bear fruit, and the first fruits are the fruit of the Spirit as found in Paul's letter to the Galatians: love, joy, peace, patience, kindness, generosity, faithfulness, gentleness, and self-control. Teresa not only wrote of a life full of the Spirit, but she lived a life full of the Spirit, giving God all the credit. A unitive/active life lived to the fullest.

Reflection with Teresa

Settle In

Take a few moments to settle in. Look around. Listen. Notice what you notice. Feel the chair supporting you and your feet on the floor. Get comfortable. Stretch a bit if that helps. Take a deep breath or two to let your body help your mind slow down. Be aware of God's

15. Teresa, *Collected Works*, 2:448.

face turned toward you in love, right here, now. *Behold God beholding you in love.* When you are settled in, move to the options below.

1. Ask the Spirit to help you become aware of a time in your life that resonated with the first and second mansions. How old were you? What was going on? What do you recall?

2. Now, how about a time when it seemed that something was impossible for you, then obedience to God's invitation made it easy. Write about that, letting yourself feel the frustration of the impossibility of the task as well as the joy of it becoming easy with God.

3. See if you can get in touch with a time in your life when the unknown of the faith journey seemed daunting. Perhaps needing to know (so valued by our culture) seemed more important, regardless of what God wanted. Write about your experience.

4. What comes to mind when you think about surrendering in humility before the living God?

5. Rest in God's presence without words, opening yourself to whatever God has for you.

6. If is true for you, conclude your reflection time with gratitude.

9

God's Gift: A Rhythm
of Work and Rest

To be sure I'm clear about the main reason I wrote this book, I want to say it again. Put simply, I want what God wants. I want people to love God back. It is the first and greatest commandment that we all long to do, and do well, but are often unsure about how. Over these chapters we have looked at others who have lived and loved well and offered a descriptive schema or pattern to help us on our own journeys.

These heroes of the faith have found the pearl of great price that is worth everything we have, this mutual exchange of love, this unitive way of living. To love the Lord your God with all your heart, soul, mind, and strength requires intentionality. This intentionality is essential for both the present moment and the future. God gives us moments throughout each day that invite us to be aware of God's love and to love God in return. That's our part of living in that unitive space. The interior fruit of the Spirit develops in us, and we respond to God's call to serve others bearing external fruit, the unitive/active way.

This chapter is to help us stay in that mutual love relationship with our Triune God, that unitive/active place, the place where we dance together. For the future it means looking at your calendar and putting times on the pages in order to be true to your heart's desire. This "rhythm of work and rest" is different for each of us and also varies depending on our season of life.

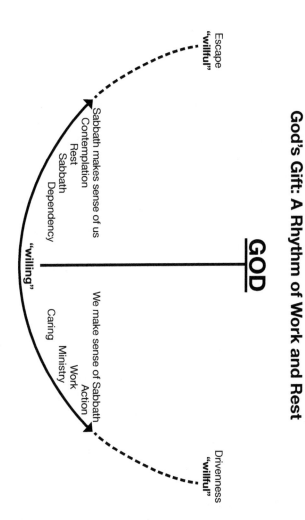

God's Gift: A Rhythm of Work and Rest

Escape
"**willful**"

Sabbath makes sense of us
Contemplation
Rest
Sabbath
Dependency

"**willing**"

GOD

We make sense of Sabbath
Action
Work
Ministry
Caring

Drivenness
"**willful**"

Please look at the Rhythm of Work and Rest diagram as one way of picturing this intentional way of living. I created this diagram in response to reading Tilden Edwards's book *Sabbath Time*. Over the course of several years, I led several weekend and day retreats sharing his wisdom and am delighted that it seems to fit well as one way to live and remain in this unitive/active way, to enjoy the dance.

God is at the top as the One to whom we listen for leading, honoring the Latin root meaning for the word "obedience"— "hyper listening." The line dropping down from God to us as we live our lives is a plumb line that gently sways "to and fro," from work to rest and back to work, depending on God's leading in each moment. Know that this rhythm of work and rest takes even greater awareness, but it is worth it. It seems essential for our survival and maybe just as importantly, it matters to God that we pay attention to God in the rhythms of our lives.

Note that the two willful extremes, escape and drivenness, are within the sound of God's whisper, but are not good settings for listening. When we are willful, we have closed our ears to any nuanced leading by God, though God does not quit revealing more of who God is and who we are; we no longer have eyes to see, ears to hear, and hearts to follow. The image that comes to mind for escape is satisfying the senses with food, drugs, possessions, or just staring blankly at a digital screen, commonly called "vegging." An image for drivenness is the tired gerbil on the treadmill running and running, going nowhere. We've all experienced both to some degree and they are not helpful and can eventually become habitual if we are not careful to pay attention to what God is revealing.

The paired words at the bottom of the diagram are simply descriptive words for the "to and fro" of the pendulum of our lives. Work and rest are the most obvious pair, taken from Genesis when God created everything in six days and then rested on the seventh. While many see the division in the amount of time, it may be more clearly honored by paying attention to God's leading. There are some seasons when we need to live much more on the work side, such as when taking care of a loved one who is ill. And there are also seasons when we need to live much more on the rest side, such as when dealing with our own illness. Sabbath and ministry are another way of saying rest and work, with the additional concept that even, or maybe especially, those in ministry need a time of sabbath. The caring of ministry or work and the dependency of rest or sabbath provide a feeling sense to go with these pairs of words. There are times when we give care as well as times when we need care—when we are dependent on others to care for us. The phrase "sabbath makes sense of us" speaks loudly to our need for this time away from demands and reminds us of the phrase in an earlier chapter that "the Sabbath has kept the Jews." Not vice versa. "We make sense of sabbath" is a phrase that relates to our engagement with the world because we have taken time to listen and therefore have a sense of direction.

Lastly, we come to the words "action and contemplation." Many have written much on comparing the two, so suffice it to say that the essential point is that the contemplation, the listening for God's leading, must come first in order to know what action God's call for me at any time is. They influence each other of course, because as Teresa of Avila said we cannot be praying for someone and not be moved to action, and we cannot be actively serving someone and not be moved to prayer. And as the unitive/active way illustrates, each hero of faith, once living in that mutual love relationship with our Triune God, once in that full to overflowing place of intimacy, could not help but overflow to others in action born of the love of God.

Note: It comes as a surprise to some that we can stay in that contemplative place, in the dance of mutual love, while we are serving. We don't need to leave God's love when we serve. If we see it as a going out to others, where is God? Isn't God everywhere, especially in others? So, as we serve, we stay; we are still at home in God's love. God invites us to live here, love here; to do both all the time. It is when we go out to try to serve on our own, without thought of God, without being willing to serve only as God leads, moving out from under the flow of the living water, that we find ourselves without

God's resources or graces, as we have moved away. God is still faithful though. God's steadfast love endures forever.

Perhaps the most clarifying word on the diagram is the word "willing" at the bottom. Our desire to "hang plumb," to stay within that smaller arc that listens well for God's whisper, is the key. The arrows on the solid line suggest the range of the swing of the pendulum. They are to encourage us to be mindful of our listening, to avoid the temptations to move to escape or drivenness. And it was fun years ago to notice that with the arrows in place, the image of where we are called to live, to make our homes in God's love, takes on the shape of an anchor.

To learn more about the difference between being willing and being willful, I recommend *Will and Spirit* by Gerald May. It has influenced my life greatly. I can hear him saying "hold things lightly" as he held out his open hand. The image for the willful life is the closed hand, even a fist. The image of the open hand holding things lightly is an encouragement to trust God more than myself, which makes sense, doesn't it? Especially if we are wanting to love God with all of who we are; we would want to honor however God is leading us instead of finding our own way.

You may want to consider these two questions. What does your current rhythm of work and rest look like? What truly rests your soul? During a spiritual directors' gathering we were brainstorming on the second question and many good options were suggested. Such things as being at the ocean, walking through the woods, contemplative prayer, music, the quiet of an empty sanctuary were all listed. It dawned on me, while looking at our list, that what truly rested my soul was God as found in each of those things. And the Scripture came to mind, "Come to me, all you who are weary and carrying heavy burdens, and I will give you rest" (Matt 11:28). What a gift! God is eager and ready to give us rest if we just come to God.

With the pace of our current culture, we can appreciate these words of Gandhi, "There is more to life than increasing its speed." We admit that it will get even faster. Technology helps in some ways, but it also has moved us toward the demand for sub-second response time, not only from our computers, but from other situations including complex issues such as relationships, healing, and grieving, just to name a few. Our fast pace is not going away; multi-tasking is essential for survival. We are living into habits that are difficult to change, especially when we are not even aware of them.

So, what is it we want? More time? If we had more, say thirty hours in a day, could we protect those extra six hours for the most important things? I doubt it. If more time isn't the answer, what is it we want? More sanity in our life perhaps? More space for reflection and replenishment? Help with discernment about what is most important? Awareness? Some tools to help us have eyes to see and ears to hear? What is it that will make our lives flow with a healthy rhythm of work and rest? What will help us live and love in God, to stay in that unitive/active place?

Tilden Edwards has written some excellent books around this idea, and *Sabbath Time*, mentioned earlier, has great wisdom. In the preface he claims that "the Christian sabbath, as a practice of receptive time that both balances and permeates our active time, has not had comprehensive, serious attention in mainstream Christian thought and practice for a long time."[1] This book was written in 1992, and even then he was saying that there is evidence of a need for honoring sabbath time, for meditation and retreat. Sabbath was never intended to be a downer. It was meant for rest. Of course, in the New Testament, over and over, Jesus heals on the Sabbath saying that the Sabbath is meant for us, not us for the Sabbath. He lived the Sabbath; it was not ended by him, but interpreted and fulfilled in the light of his mission.

My hope is that you're getting the connection, recognizing the unitive/active way. This dance, this unitive/active way, may best be lived by finding your own rhythm of work and rest that depends totally on listening for God, the Great Whisperer, so that you can be willing in all you do to honor however God leads you.

In sessions of spiritual direction, I often hear of how exhausted people are and how they long for rest. Sometimes I try to help

1. Edwards, *Sabbath Time*, 8.

them be aware of God's presence with them and God's awareness and care for them—to know that God's face is always turned toward them, even when they are not finding time to turn their faces toward God. Sometimes I can help them to glimpse the light at the end of the tunnel, and together we make a note with hopes of planning a restful retreat when we get closer to the light.

Let's talk about rest. Not just catching a nap but a real quality of resting which can be the very ground of our true work. Truly resting from our work can leave us empty of striving. In that emptiness there is space to let in the divine whispers that are always moving through our souls. The spirit-breath can move us to realize our sometimes awesome, sometimes playful communion with what is and the One who radiantly lives through what is. The spirit-breath can also shape images in us that inspire our work. These may be very simple inner movements, such as wanting to write someone a letter, bring some items to the clothing drive for the poor, do something for a family member, or tend the garden. The whispered ideas may also plant seeds for larger movements within—a new direction in our lives, a creative idea for the workplace, a vision for a spiritual community, an organized challenge for some social injustice.

This kind of rest can be called visioning rest, or perhaps it is better called "listening rest," when we let go of our agendas, empty ourselves of any plan, and open ourselves to whatever the Spirit might bring. Hopefully this concept is a reminder of the purgative way, letting God make space in us, and our part is to surrender. This kind of time is part of my story about how The Anchorage was born in a listening retreat.

Can you see how this kind of rest could be just what is needed to be able to remain in the unitive/active place without moving into attempting to do it all by yourself? However, there is a need to be careful. For when we are moved by these whispers into outward work, the temptation is to stop listening and take over the activity, to move away from our home in God's love. That leads to other temptations, such as becoming attached to the work having a predetermined result or worrying about how others may be judging what we're doing. Then the work becomes more "self" work than it needs to be, more our work than God's work. We can lose touch with the ongoing whispers that come from continually "resting" in the divine source of our inspired work.

By this I mean the value of opening what we are deciding, feeling, and doing again and again during the day to the Great Whisperer. In that space of opening, I have found that my consciousness realizes its connectedness and availability to the divine Consciousness. In my relative emptiness, I breathe in the qualities of a larger confidence, energy, and loving wisdom that I want to breathe out into my work and thus join the great work of God in ongoing creation. My own anxieties can fill up my empty presence before God. And even when I am widely open to the Spirit's presence, often I am not given anything clear in that opening. But, in my very desire to lean close to the Spirit's breath, I sense that I am freed from my own separating narrowness a little, freed for something larger, something of God, to live through me.

I'm sure we all could give our own witness to the fruit of such "resting" into work, however small it may seem at times. Could it be that the Spirit's invisible breath wants to waft invisible goodness/Godness through us in countless little ways all through the day? All that is needed from us is our willingness to restfully open into the Spirit's active presence. I believe our best work flows from our spacious resting in God, in our intimate mutual love relationship, our graced dance.

Spending this kind of open time with God leads us to ask the next question. It may be one you have asked before, but whether it is a new question or one you've wrestled with for years, it needs to be asked now. What does God want? What do you think God wants as far as the rhythm of work and rest in our lives? First, we need to take a few minutes to consider what image of God is our prevalent image. If you see God as a stern taskmaster who is never satisfied with your work no matter how hard you try, your answer will be that God wants us to work ourselves to exhaustion. If you see God as abusive and uncaring, you will say God just wants to get the job done.

From my own experience of hearing the experiences of others and from reading many books, it seems to me that the more we learn who God is, the more we become aware of how much God loves us and longs for us to be together, to do things together.

Beginning at the beginning, in Genesis God walks in the garden with Adam and Eve—God wants a relationship. But the most prevalent image of God in the Old Testament that I see is the God who looks upon the Israelites in their captivity in Egypt and says to Moses, "I have observed the misery of my people who are in Egypt; I have heard their cry on account of their taskmasters. Indeed, I know their sufferings, and I have come down to deliver them from the Egyptians, and to bring them up out of that land to a good and broad land, a land flowing with milk and honey. . ." (Exod 3:7–8). This passage was part of my call to ministry.

Recall with me the many Old Testament passages when God begins his words with these words, "I am the Lord your God, who brought you out of the land of Egypt" (Exod 20:2; Lev 26:13; Deut 5:6, to name a few). If that is the main way God wants to be known, doesn't that say something about God's nature? God wants us to be free of whatever oppresses us, whatever binds us, whatever hinders our freedom to live as fully loved sons and daughters.

The New Testament follows with the same message. Jesus becomes one of us so that we might know who God is. What phrase is used often throughout the New Testament about Jesus? "When he saw the crowds, he had compassion on them, for they were harassed and helpless, they were like sheep without a shepherd" (Matt 9:36). Jesus, as the expression of God, of the Trinity, can't help loving people. This image of a loving and caring God is the image that continues to ring true to me. Not a saccharine, sappy love that is just an emotional high, but a love that will not let me go in the toughest times of my life.

As we ponder what *that* God's longings are for us, the response is that God longs to give us rest, to free us from our oppressions. How does God want to do that? The words from Matthew's Gospel, "Come to me," say it well. This invitation from Jesus implies we are away. We need to be near Christ to find this rest. Is there anything we need to do before we can come to God? Good things (school, service, work) may take us away from the best (God).

There is nothing needed except a willingness, and God will even help with that. I invite you to let your calendar be part of what you bring to your listening time. Being intentional about your time with God takes some planning and some letting go of lesser things. There are many ways to live into this graced space, as you may have found, but we must ponder what is needed when in this season of life. What rhythm will fill you to overflowing with the love of God for yourself first and then, loving God with God's very love, create that mutuality of love that overflows to others?

From my own journey, after making the thirty-day spiritual exercises at the Jesuit Center for Spiritual Growth in Wernersville, Pennsylvania, in 2001, I went back annually for an eight-day retreat to honor the suggestion for ongoing growth. You may want to listen for your own rhythm as God leads. You may want to consider a week a year, a weekend a quarter, a day a month, a half day a week, an hour a day, setting aside time to be with God. What rhythm is God calling you to now in this season of your life?

A dream put into my heart by God years ago is to have a place where people can take a vacation with God, be close enough to walk to meet with me for processing their prayer daily, and still have an individual cabin far enough away from others that they could play their guitar, sing, or cry without bothering anyone. The vision includes a small lake with cabins in the surrounding woods. The lake helps to make sense of the name The Anchorage. I'm trusting God with it all. Thank you for your prayer, as God leads.

To conclude, if you are encouraged to make your home in God's love, to give the first and greatest commandment its place as first in your life, honoring that it is all God's grace, then my sense is that God's purpose has been accomplished in writing this book together. When we ponder the lives and teachings of Augustine, Bernard, Catherine, Ignatius, Calvin, and Teresa, we become aware of their love relationship with God. It is not just central in their lives, or what their lives are all about; it is evident that everything they accomplished was because they were abiding in God. Each one in his or her own unique way had taken to heart this first and greatest commandment to love God with all their heart, soul, mind, and strength. They were willing to be the branch and let Jesus be the vine. They made their home in God's love.

This invitation is for each of us, as well, as we listen for God's call. God does not say that the way will be easy but does say that we never go alone. God wants to increase our capacity to receive all that God wants to give, to be the branch attached to the vine, to live the unitive/active life, to hang plumb, listening for the Great Whisperer, to participate with God. So, consider this invitation: Make time to listen, to hear what God wants to say to you; to receive all that God longs to give you. Listen for God's leading, and find a rhythm that provides you with time to "come away—anchor deep!"

Whether you stay home or come away, the heart of the matter is that God is inviting you and longs to make your joy full. God invites us all saying, "Make your home in my love; live in my joy."

Reflection on God's Gift:
A Rhythm of Work and Rest

Settle In

Take a few moments to settle in. Look around. Listen. Notice what you notice. Feel the chair supporting you and your feet on the floor. Get comfortable. Stretch a bit if that helps. Take a deep breath or two to let your body help your mind slow down. Be aware of God's face turned toward you in love, right here, now. *Behold God beholding you in love.* When you are settled in, move to the options below.

1. Looking over your journal for the chapters in this book, are there any areas that seem to be directed specifically to you? Thoughts that resonated deeply with who you are? Do you find yourself wanting some undistracted time to go even deeper? Write some about that.

2. What resistance comes up in you as you ponder the possibility of putting such time on your calendar? Logistics usually can be figured out, as God is very creative. Listen with the ear of your heart for God's invitation and for God's leading.

3. Enjoy some reflection time just to be with God in openness. Notice how God comes to you—as Abba, Amma, Jesus, the Risen Christ, Spirit, Rock, Shepherd, and on and on. Let God love you and then love God back; a simple "I love you," will do.

4. Ask God for the grace to surrender all. To trust when the way isn't clear.

5. Close your reflection time with gratitude if it is true for you—and perhaps with a wink to God that you'll be back. You might look for God's wink in return.

Bibliography

Armstrong, Regis J., and Ingrid J. Peterson. *The Franciscan Tradition*. Spirituality in History. Collegeville, MN: Liturgical, 2010.

Augustine. *Augustine of Hippo: Selected Writings*. Translated by Mary T. Clark. Classics of Western Spirituality. New York: Paulist, 1984.

———. *The City of God*. Translated by Marcus Dods. New York: Modern Library, 2000.

———. *Confessions*. Translated by Henry Chadwick. New York: Oxford University Press, 1998.

———. *Late Have I Loved Thee: Selected Writings of Saint Augustine On Love*. Edited by John F. Thornton and Susan B. Varenne. New York: Vintage, 2006.

———. *Love One Another, My Friends: Saint Augustine's Homilies on the First Letter of John*. Edited by John Leinenweber. San Francisco: Harper & Row, 1989.

———. *On Christian Teaching*. Translated by R. P. H. Green. New York: Oxford University Press, 1997.

———. *Sermons III/11*. Translated by Edmund Hill. *The Works of Saint Augustine: A Translation for the 21st Century*. New York: New City, 1997.

Barclay, William. *The Gospel of John*. Daily Study Bible Series 2. Philadelphia: Westminster, 1956.

Battles, Ford Lewis, ed. *The Piety of John Calvin: An Anthology Illustrative of the Spirituality of the Reformer*. Grand Rapids: Baker, 1978.

Bennett, Jana Marguerite, and Melissa Musick Nussbaum. *Free to Leave, Free to Stay: Fruits of the Spirit and Church Choice*. Eugene, OR: Cascade, 2009.

Bergen, Jacqueline Syrup, and Marie Schwan. *Praying with Ignatius of Loyola*. Winona, MN: Saint Mary's, 1991.

Bernard of Clairvaux. *On the Song of Songs I*. Translated by Kilian Walsh. Spencer, MA: Cistercian, 1971.

———. *On the Song of Songs III*. Translated by Kilian Walsh and Irene M. Edmonds. Kalamazoo, MI: Cistercian, 1979.

————. *On the Song of Songs IV.* Translated by Irene M. Edmonds. Kalamazoo, MI: Cistercian, 1980.

————. *Talks on the Song of Songs: Bernard of Clairvaux.* Edited by Bernard Bangley. Brewster, MA: Paraclete, 2002.

Brady, Bernard V. *Christian Love: How Christians through the Ages Have Understood Love.* Washington, DC: Georgetown University Press, 2003.

Brown, Peter. *Augustine of Hippo: A Biography.* Rev. ed. Los Angeles: University of California Press, 2000.

Brown, Raymond E. *The Gospel and Epistles of John: A Concise Commentary.* Collegeville, MN: Liturgical, 1988.

Bruteau, Beatrice. *Radical Optimism: Practical Spirituality in an Uncertain World.* Boulder, CO: Sentient, 1993.

Burke, Kevin, ed. *Pedro Arrupe: Essential Writings.* Modern Spiritual Masters Series. Maryknoll, NY: Orbis, 2005.

Burnaby, John. *Amor Dei: A Study of the Religion of St. Augustine.* London: Hodder & Stoughton, 1938.

Burrows, Ruth. *Interior Castle Explored: St. Teresa's Teaching on the Life of Deep Union with God.* London: Sheed and Ward, 1981.

Calvin, John. *Calvin: Institutes of the Christian Religion.* Vol. 20 and 21. Edited by John T. McNeill. Translated and indexed by Ford Lewis Battles. Louisville: Westminster John Knox, 1960.

————. *Commentary on the Gospel According to John.* Vol. I & II. Translated by William Pringle. Grand Rapids: Eerdmans, 1956.

————. *The Epistle of Paul the Apostle to the Hebrews and the First and Second Epistles of St. Peter.* Edited by David W. Torrance and Thomas F. Torrance. Translated by William B. Johnston. Calvin's New Testament Commentaries. Grand Rapids: Eerdmans, 1963.

————. *The Epistles of Paul the Apostle to the Romans and Thessalonians.* Edited by David W. Torrance and Thomas F. Torrance. Translated by Ross Mackenzie. Calvin's New Testament Commentaries. Grand Rapids: Eerdmans, 1960.

————. *John Calvin: Writings on Pastoral Piety.* Edited by Elsie Anne McKee. Classics of Western Spirituality. New York: Paulist, 2001.

————. *Letters of John Calvin.* Vol. I, III, IV. Edited by Jules Bonnet. Translated by Marcus Robert Gilchrist. New York: Burt Franklin, 1972.

Canlis, Julie. *Calvin's Ladder.* Grand Rapids, MI: Eerdmans, 2010.

Capalbo, Battistina, compiler. *Praying with Saint Teresa.* Grand Rapids: Eerdmans, 1997.

Casey, Michael. *Athirst for God: Spiritual Desire in Bernard of Clairvaux's Sermons on the Song of Songs.* Kalamazoo, MI: Cistercian, 1987.

Catherine of Siena. *Catherine of Siena: The Dialogue.* Translated by Suzanne Noffke. Classics of Western Spirituality. New York: Paulist, 1980.

————. *Little Talks with God.* Edited by Henry L. Carrigan Jr. Brewster, MA: Paraclete, 2007.

———. "Arriving at Pure and Generous Love." In *Praying with Your Whole Heart*. Brewster, MA: Paraclete, 2014.

Christensen, Bernhard. *The Inward Pilgrimage: Spiritual Classics from Augustine to Bonhoeffer*. Minneapolis: Augsburg, 1976.

Dyckman, Katherine, et al. *The Spiritual Exercises Reclaimed: Uncovering Liberating Possibilities for Women*. New York: Paulist, 2001.

Edwards, Tilden. *Sabbath Time*. Nashville: Upper Room, 1992.

Egan, Keith J., ed. *Carmelite Prayer: A Tradition for the 21st Century*. New York: Paulist, 2003.

Ellsberg, Robert. *Blessed among All Women: Women Saints, Prophets, and Witnesses for Our Time*. New York: Crossroad, 2005.

Evans, G. R., ed. *The Medieval Theologians*. Oxford: Blackwell, 2001.

Fallon, Michael. *The Four Gospels: An Introductory Commentary*. Sydney: Catholic Adult Education Centre, 1980.

Fleming, David. "The First Principle and Foundation." In *Hearts on Fire: Praying with Jesuits*, edited by Michael Harter. St. Louis: Institute of Jesuit Sources, 1993.

Forbes, F. A. *St. Teresa of Avila: Reformer of Carmel*. Rockford, IL: TAN, 1998.

Foster, Richard J., and Gayle D. Beebe. *Longing for God: Seven Paths of Christian Devotion*. Downers Grove: InterVarsity, 2009.

Galilea, Segundo. *The Future of Our Past: The Spanish Mystics Speak to Contemporary Spirituality*. Notre Dame, IN: Ave Maria, 1985.

———. *Temptation and Discernment*. Translated by Stephen-Joseph Ross. Washington, DC: Institute of Carmelite Studies, 1996.

Gilson, Etienne. *The Mystical Theology of Saint Bernard*. Translated by A. H. C. Downes. New York: Sheed and Ward, 1953.

Green, Thomas H. *A Vacation with the Lord: A Personal, Directed Retreat Based on the Spiritual Exercises of St Ignatius of Loyola*. San Francisco: Ignatius, 2000.

Groeschel, Benedict J. *The Journey Toward God*. Ann Arbor: Charis, 2000.

———. *Spiritual Passages: The Psychology of Spiritual Development*. New York: Crossroad, 2005.

Harrington, Wilfrid J. *John: Spiritual Theologian; The Jesus of John*. Dublin: Columba, 1999.

Haughton, Rosemary. *The Passionate God*. New York: Paulist, 1981.

Hayes, Mark. "To Love Our God." Text adapted by John Parker. Chapel Hill, NC: Hinshaw Music, 1997.

Heimsoeth, Heinz. *The Six Great Themes of Western Metaphysics and the End of the Middle Ages*. Detroit: Wayne State University Press, 1994.

Howard, Wilburt F., and Arthur John Gossip. "The Gospel According to John." In *The Interpreter's Bible* 8. New York: Abingdon, 1952.

Ignatius of Loyola. *Ignatius of Loyola: Spiritual Exercises and Selected Works*. Edited by George E. Ganss. Classics of Western Spirituality. New York: Paulist, 1991.

————. *The Spiritual Exercises of Saint Ignatius: A Translation and Commentary.* Edited by George E. Ganss. Chicago: Loyola University Press, 1992.

————. *The Spiritual Exercises of St. Ignatius.* Translated by Anthony Mottola. New York: Image, 1989.

————. *The Spiritual Exercises of St. Ignatius.* Translated by Louis J. Puhl. New York: Vintage, 2000.

Ivens, Michael. *Understanding the Spiritual Exercises.* Trowbridge, Wiltshire: Cromwell, 1998.

Johnson, Merwyn S. *Resource Material for the Study of Christian Theology and Ministry.* Self-published, 2005.

Kerr, Hugh T., ed. *By John Calvin.* An Association Press Reflection Book. New York: Association, 1960.

Kessler, Michael, and Christian Sheppard, eds. *Mystics: Presence and Aporia.* Chicago: University of Chicago Press, 2003.

King, Ursula. *Christian Mystics: The Spiritual Heart of the Christian Tradition.* New York: Simon & Schuster, 1998.

Koester, Craig R. *Symbolism in the Fourth Gospel: Meaning, Mystery, Community.* Minneapolis: Fortress, 1995.

Kozlowski, Joseph Paul. *Spiritual Direction and Spiritual Directors: St. Francis de Sales, St. Teresa of Avila, Thomas a Kempis and St. John of the Cross.* Santa Barbara: Queenship, 1998.

Leclercq, Jean. "Introduction." In *Bernard of Clairvaux: Selected Works.* Classics of Western Spirituality. New York: Paulist, 1987.

LeFevre, Perry D., ed. *The Prayers of Kierkegaard.* Chicago: University of Chicago Press, 1956.

Lerner, Harriet. *The Dance of Fear.* New York: HarperCollins, 2005.

Luibheid, Colm, trans. *Pseudo-Dionysius: The Complete Works.* Classics of Western Spirituality. New York: Paulist, 1987.

Macquarrie, John. *Two Worlds Are Ours: An Introduction to Christian Mysticism.* Minneapolis: Fortress, 2005.

Maloney, George A. *An Eight-Day Retreat: Alone with the Alone.* Notre Dame, IN: Ave Maria, 1982.

————. *Entering into the Heart of Jesus: Meditations on the Indwelling Trinity in St. John's Gospel.* New York: Alba, 1988.

Matthew, Iain. *The Impact of God: Soundings from St. John of the Cross.* London: Hodder & Stoughton, 1995.

May, Gerald G. *The Awakened Heart: Opening Yourself to the Love You Need.* New York: HarperCollins, 1991.

McCabe, Maureen F. *I Am the Way: Stages of Prayer in Saint Bernard.* Trappist, KY: Cistercian, 2012.

McGinn, Bernard. *The Doctors of the Church: Thirty-three Men and Women Who Shaped Christianity.* New York: Crossroad, 1999.

————. *The Presence of God: A History of Western Christian Mysticism.* Vol. 1, *The Foundations of Mysticism: Origins to the Fifth Century.* New York: Crossroad, 1991.

————. *The Presence of God: A History of Western Christian Mysticism.* Vol. 2, *The Growth of Mysticism: Gregory the Great through the 12th Century.* New York: Crossroad, 1994.

————. *The Presence of God: A History of Western Christian Mysticism.* Vol. 3, *The Flowering of Mysticism: Men and Women in the New Mysticism.* New York: Crossroad, 1998.

McGinn, Bernard, and Patricia Ferris McGinn. *Early Christian Mystics: The Divine Vision of the Spiritual Masters.* New York: Crossroad, 2003.

Meade, Catherine M. *My Nature Is Fire: Saint Catherine of Siena.* New York: Alba, 1991.

Meeks, Wayne A., ed. *HarperCollins Study Bible.* New York: HarperCollins, 1993.

Morello, Sam Anthony. *Lectio Divina and the Practice of Teresian Prayer.* Washington, DC: Institute of Carmelite Studies, 1994.

Muto, Susan. *Where Lovers Meet: Inside the Interior Castle.* Washington, DC: Institute of Carmelite Studies, 2008.

Nygren, Anders. *Agape and Eros.* Translated by Philip S. Watson. Philadelphia: Westminster, 1953.

Obbard, Elizabeth Ruth, ed. *Medieval Women Mystics.* Hyde Park, NY: New City, 2002.

O'Donoghue, Noel. *Adventures in Prayer: Reflections on St. Teresa of Avila, St. John of the Cross and St. Therese of Lisieux.* New York: Burns & Oates, 2004.

Olin, John C. *A Reformation Debate: John Calvin & Jacopo Sadoleto; Sadoleto's Letter to the Genevans and Calvin's Reply.* Grand Rapids: Baker, 1966.

Pascal, Blaise. *Pensees.* Suffolk: Penguin, 1995.

Payne, Steven, ed. *Paul-Marie of the Cross: Carmelite Spirituality in the Teresian Tradition.* Translated by Kathryn Sullivan. Washington, DC: Institute of Carmelite Studies, 1997.

Peers, E. Allison, ed. *The Life of Teresa of Jesus: The Autobiography of St. Teresa of Avila.* Garden City, NY: Image, 1960.

Peterson, Eugene. *The Message.* Colorado Springs: NavPress, 2002.

Pius, Pope, XII, "Doctor Mellifluus: Encyclical of Pope Pius XII on Saint Bernard of Clairvaux." http://w2.vatican.va/content/pius-xii/en/encyclicals/documents/hf_p-xii_enc_24051953_doctor-mellifluus.html.

The Presbyterian Hymnal. Louisville: Westminster John Knox, 1990.

Raitt, Jill, et al. *Christian Spirituality: High Middle Ages and Reformation.* New York: Crossroad, 1987.

Rist, John M. *Augustine: Ancient Thought Baptized.* New York: Cambridge University Press, 1994.

Robson, Michael. *The Franciscans in the Middle Ages.* Woodbridge: Boydell, 2006.

Rohr, Richard. *The Naked Now: Learning to See as the Mystics See.* New York: Crossroad, 2009.

Rohrbach, Peter. *Conversation with Christ: The Teaching of St. Teresa of Avila about Personal Prayer.* Rockford, IL: TAN, 1980.

Schaef, Anne Wilson. *When Society Becomes an Addict.* San Francisco: Harper & Row, 1987.

Schemel, George J., and Judith A. Roemer. *Beyond Individuation to Discipleship: A Directory for Those Who Give the Spiritual Exercises of St. Ignatius.* Scranton, PA: Self-published, 1999.

Seelaus, Vilma. *Distractions in Prayer: Blessing or Curse?* New York: Alba, 2005.

Shannon, William H. *Silence on Fire: The Prayer of Awareness.* New York: Crossroad, 1993.

Smith, D. Moody. *Interpreting the Gospels for Preaching.* Philadelphia: Fortress, 1980.

Tamburello, Dennis E. *Union with Christ: John Calvin and the Mysticism of St. Bernard.* Louisville: Westminster John Knox, 1994.

Teresa of Avila. *The Collected Works of St. Teresa of Avila.* Vol. 1. Edited by Kieran Kavanaugh and Otilio Rodriguez. Washington, DC: Institute of Carmelite Studies, 1987.

———. *The Collected Works of St. Teresa of Avila.* Vol. 2. Edited by Kieran Kavanaugh and Otilio Rodriguez. Washington, DC: Institute of Carmelite Studies, 1980.

———. *The Collected Works of St. Teresa of Avila.* Vol. 3. Edited by Kieran Kavanaugh and Otilio Rodriguez. Washington, DC: Institute of Carmelite Studies, 1985.

———. *The Interior Castle.* Translated by the Benedictines of Stanbrook. Rockford, IL: TAN, 1997.

———. *The Way of Perfection: A Study Edition.* Edited by Kieran Kavanaugh. Washington, DC: Institute of Carmelite Studies, 2000.

———. *The Way of Prayer.* Edited by Kieran Kavanaugh. Hyde Park, NY: New City, 2003.

Tetlow, Joseph A. *Choosing Christ in the World.* St. Louis: Institute of Jesuit Sources, 1999.

Van Kaam, Adrian. *The Mystery of Transforming Love.* Denville, NJ: Dimension, 1982.

Vest, Norvene. *Gathered in the Word.* Nashville: Upper Room, 1996.

Von Speyr, Adrienne. *The Farewell Discourses: Meditations on John 13–17.* Translated by E. A. Nelson. San Francisco: Ignatius, 1987.

Welch, John. *The Carmelite Way: An Ancient Path for Today's Pilgrim.* New York: Paulist, 1996.

———. *Spiritual Pilgrims: Carl Jung and Teresa of Avila.* New York: Paulist, 1982.

Williams, Rowan. *Why Study the Past? The Quest for the Historical Church.* Grand Rapids: Eerdmans, 2005.

Wright, N. T. *John for Everyone, Part 2.* New York: SPCK, 2002.

Wright, Wendy. *The Essential Spirituality Handbook.* Liguori, MO: Liguori, 2009.

Wuellner, Flora Slosson. *Release: Healing from Wounds of Family, Church and Community.* Nashville: Upper Room, 1996.

CPSIA information can be obtained
at www.ICGtesting.com
Printed in the USA
JSHW021508031219
2751JS00003B/12

9 781532 684043